D0917354

GRAPHIC DESIGN

THE NEW BASICS

SECOND EDITION, REVISED AND EXPANDED

ELLEN LUPTON AND JENNIFER COLE PHILLIPS

Princeton Architectural Press, New York and

Maryland Institute College of Art, Baltimore

Published by
Princeton Architectural Press
A division of Chronicle Books LLC
70 West 36th Street, New York, NY 10018
papress.com

© 2008, 2015 Princeton Architectural Press
All rights reserved
Printed and bound in China by
Toppan Leefung
25 24 23   10 9

No part of this book may be used or
reproduced in any manner without written
permission from the publisher, except in
the context of reviews.

Every reasonable attempt has been made
to identify owners of copyright. Errors or
omissions will be corrected in subsequent
editions.

Library of Congress Cataloging-in-Publication Data
Lupton, Ellen, author.
 Graphic design : the new basics / Ellen Lupton and
Jennifer Cole Phillips. — Second Edition, Revised and
Expanded.
 261 pages ; 23 cm
 Includes bibliographical references and index.
 ISBN 978-1-61689-325-5 (hardcover : alk. paper)
 ISBN 978-1-61689-332-3 (paperback : alk. paper)
 1. Graphic arts. I. Phillips, Jennifer C., 1960– author.
II. Title.
 NC997.L87 2015
 741.6—dc23
                              2014046286

For Maryland Institute College of Art

Book Design
Ellen Lupton and Jennifer Cole Phillips

Contributing Faculty
Ken Barber
Kristian Bjørnard
Kimberly Bost
Jeremy Botts
Corinne Botz
Bernard Canniffe
Nancy Froehlich
Brockett Horne
Tal Leming
Ellen Lupton
Al Maskeroni
Sandra Maxa
Ryan McCabe
Abbott Miller
Kiel Mutschelknaus
Jennifer Cole Phillips
James Ravel
Zvezdana Stojmirovic
Nolen Strals
Mike Weikert
Bruce Willen
Yeohyun Ahn

Visiting Artists
Marian Bantjes
Nicholas Blechman
Alicia Cheng
Peter Cho
Malcolm Grear
David Plunkert
C. E. B. Reas
Paul Sahre
Jan van Toorn
Rick Valicenti

For Princeton Architectural Press

Editors
Clare Jacobson and Nicola Brower

Special thanks to
Janet Behning, Erin Cain, Megan Carey,
Carina Cha, Andrea Chlad, Tom Cho,
Barbara Darko, Benjamin English,
Russell Fernandez, Jan Cigliano Hartman,
Jan Haux, Mia Johnson, Diane Levinson,
Jennifer Lippert, Katharine Myers,
Jaime Nelson, Rob Shaeffer, Sara Stemen,
Marielle Suba, Kaymar Thomas, Paul Wagner,
Joseph Weston, and Janet Wong of Princeton
Architectural Press
—Kevin C. Lippert, publisher

Contents

Foreword

Ellen Lupton and Jennifer Cole Phillips

This book is a guide to visual form-making, showing designers how to build richness and complexity around simple relationships. We created the first edition of this book in 2008 because we didn't see anything quite like it for today's students and young designers: a concise, contemporary guide to two-dimensional design. Since its release, *Graphic Design: The New Basics* has reached an enthusiastic audience around the world. Everywhere we go, we meet educators and young designers who have used the book and learned something from it.

What's new in this volume? You will find updated and expanded content throughout the book, reflecting new ideas emerging in our classrooms at Maryland Institute College of Art (MICA). The most important addition to this volume, however, is an entirely new opening chapter devoted to "formstorming," a term originated by Jennifer Cole Phillips. Formstorming is a set of structured techniques for generating visual solutions to graphic design challenges. We open the book with this chapter in order to plunge our readers directly into the act of visual invention.

As educators with decades of combined experience in graduate and undergraduate teaching, we have witnessed the design world change and change again in response to new technologies. When we were students ourselves in the 1980s, classic books such as Armin Hofmann's *Graphic Design Manual* (published in 1965) had begun to lose their relevance within the restless and shifting design scene. Postmodernism was on the rise, and abstract design exercises seemed out of step with the interest at that time in appropriation and historicism.

During the 1990s, design educators became caught in the pressure to teach (and learn) software, and many of us struggled to balance technical skills with visual and critical thinking. Form sometimes got lost along the way, as design methodologies moved away from universal visual concepts toward a more anthropological understanding of design as a constantly changing flow of cultural sensibilities.

This book addresses the gap between software and visual thinking. By focusing on form, we have re-embraced the pioneering work of modernist design educators, from Josef Albers and László Moholy-Nagy at the Bauhaus to Armin Hofmann and some of our own great teachers, including Malcolm Grear.

We initiated this project when we noticed that our students were not at ease building concepts abstractly. They were adept at working and reworking pop-culture vocabularies, but they were less comfortable manipulating scale, rhythm, color, hierarchy, grids, and diagrammatic relationships.

This is a book for students and emerging designers, and it is illustrated primarily with student work, produced within graduate and undergraduate design studios. Our school, MICA, has been our laboratory. Numerous faculty and scores of students participated in our brave experiment. The work shown on these pages is varied and diverse, reflecting an organic range of skill levels and sensibilities. Unless otherwise noted, all the student examples were generated in the context of MICA's courses; a few projects originate from schools we visited or where our own graduate alumni are teaching.

Our student contributors come from China, India, Japan, Korea, Puerto Rico, Trinidad, Zimbabwe, a wide range of US states, and many other places. The book was manufactured in China and published with Princeton Architectural Press in New York City. It was thus created in a global context. The work presented within its pages is energized by the diverse backgrounds of its producers, whose creativity is shaped by their cultural identities as well as by their unique life experiences. A common thread that draws all these people together in one place is design.

The majority of student work featured here comes from the course we teach together at MICA, the Graphic Design MFA Studio. Our MFA program's first publishing venture was the book *D.I.Y.: Design It Yourself* (2006), directed at general readers who want to use design in their own lives. We have published a series of other titles since then, including *Indie Publishing* (2009), *Graphic Design Thinking* (2010), and *Type on Screen* (2014). These books are researched and produced under the aegis of MICA's Center for Design Thinking, an umbrella for organizing the college's diverse efforts in the area of design education research.

Complementing the student work included in this book are examples from contemporary professional practice that demonstrate visually rich design approaches. Many of the designers featured, including Marian Bantjes, Alicia Cheng, Peter Cho, Malcolm Grear, David Plunkert, C.E.B. Reas, Paul Sahre, Rick Valicenti, and Jan van Toorn, have worked with our students as visiting artists at MICA. Some conducted special workshops, whose results are included in this volume.

Graphic Design: The New Basics lays out the elements of a visual language whose forms are employed by individuals, institutions, and communities that are increasingly connected in a global society. We hope the book will inspire more thought and creativity in the years ahead.

Acknowledgments

The first edition of this book constituted my degree project in the Doctorate in Communication Design program at the University of Baltimore. I thank my advisors, Stuart Moulthrop, Sean Carton, and Amy Pointer. I also thank my colleagues at MICA, including Samuel Hoi, president; Ray Allen, provost; Gwynne Keathley, vice provost for research and graduate studies; Brockett Horne, chair, Graphic Design BFA; and my longtime friend and collaborator, Jennifer Cole Phillips. Special thanks go to the dozens of students who contributed work.

Editors Clare Jacobson, Nicola Brower, and the team at Princeton Architectural Press made the book real.

My family is an inspiration, especially my parents Bill, Lauren, Mary Jane, and Ken; my children Jay and Ruby; my sisters Julia and Michelle; and my husband Abbott.

Ellen Lupton

My contribution to this book is dedicated to Malcolm Grear, mentor and friend, who taught me to approach design from the inside out, and instilled an appetite for invention and formal rigor.

The culture at MICA is a joy in which to work, thanks in large part to the vision and support of our past president, Fred Lazarus; our new president, Samuel Hoi; provost Ray Allen; vice provost for research and graduate studies Gwynne Keathley; and our talented faculty colleagues. Deep respect and thanks to our students for their commitment and contributions. Heartfelt gratitude goes to my friend and close collaborator, Ellen Lupton, for raising the bar with grace and generosity.

I am thankful for the support of my family and close friends, especially my parents Ann and Jack; and my sisters Lanie and Jodie.

Jennifer Cole Phillips

Back to the Bauhaus

Ellen Lupton

The idea of searching out a shared framework in which to invent and organize visual content dates back to the origins of modern graphic design. In the 1920s, institutions such as the Bauhaus in Germany explored design as a universal, perceptually based "language of vision," a concept that continues to shape design education today around the world.

This book reflects on that vital tradition in light of profound shifts in technology and global social life. Whereas the Bauhaus promoted rational solutions through planning and standardization, designers and artists today are drawn to idiosyncrasy, customization, and sublime accidents as well as to standards and norms. The modernist preference for reduced, simplified forms now coexists with a desire to build systems that yield unexpected results. Today, the impure, the contaminated, and the hybrid hold as much allure as forms that are sleek and perfected. Visual thinkers often seek to spin out intricate results from simple rules or concepts rather than reduce an image or idea to its simplest parts.

The Bauhaus Legacy In the 1920s, faculty at the Bauhaus and other schools analyzed form in terms of basic geometric elements. They believed this language would be understandable to everyone, grounded in the universal instrument of the eye.

Bauhaus faculty pursued this idea from different points of view. Wassily Kandinsky called for the creation of a "dictionary of elements" and a universal visual "grammar" in his Bauhaus textbook *Point and Line to Plane*. His colleague László Moholy-Nagy sought to uncover a rational vocabulary ratified by a shared society and a common humanity. Courses taught by Josef Albers emphasized systematic thinking over personal intuition, objectivity over emotion.

Albers and Moholy-Nagy forged the use of new media and new materials. They saw that art and design were being transformed by technology—photography, film, and mass production. And yet their ideas remained profoundly humanistic, always asserting the role of the individual over the absolute authority of any system or method. Design, they argued, is never reducible to its function or to a technical description.

Since the 1940s, numerous educators have refined and expanded on the Bauhaus approach, from Moholy-Nagy and Gyorgy Kepes at the New Bauhaus in Chicago; to Johannes Itten, Max Bill, and Gui Bonsiepe at the Ulm School in Germany; to Emil Ruder and Armin Hofmann in Switzerland; to the "new typographies" of Wolfgang Weingart, Dan Friedman, and Katherine McCoy in Switzerland and the United States. Each of these revolutionary educators articulated structural approaches to design from distinct and original perspectives.

Some of them also engaged in the postmodern rejection of universal communication. According to postmodernism, which emerged in the 1960s, it is futile to look for inherent meaning in an image or object because people will bring their own cultural biases and personal experiences to the process of interpretation. As postmodernism itself became a dominant ideology in the 1980s and '90s, in both the academy and in the marketplace, the design process got mired in the act of referencing cultural styles or tailoring messages to narrowly defined communities.

The New Basics Designers at the Bauhaus believed not only in a universal way of *describing* visual form, but also in its universal *significance*. Reacting against that belief, postmodernism discredited formal experiment as a primary component of thinking and making in the visual arts. Formal study was considered to be tainted by its link to universalistic ideologies. This book recognizes a difference between description and interpretation, between a potentially universal language of making and the universality of meaning.

Today, software designers have realized the Bauhaus goal of describing (but not interpreting) the language of vision in a universal way. Software organizes visual material into menus of properties, parameters, filters, and so on, creating tools that are universal in their social ubiquity, cross-disciplinarity, and descriptive power. Photoshop, for example, is a systematic study of the features of an image (its contrast, size, color model, and so on). InDesign and QuarkXpress are structural explorations of typography: they are software machines for controlling leading, alignment, spacing, and column structures as well as image placement and page layout.

In the aftermath of the Bauhaus, textbooks of basic design have re-turned again and again to elements such as point, line, plane, texture, and color, organized by principles of scale, contrast, movement, rhythm, and balance. This book revisits those concepts as well as looking at some of the new universals emerging today.

Transparency and Layers The Google Earth interface allows users to manipulate the transparency of overlays placed over satellite photographs of Earth. Here, Hurricane Katrina hovers over the Gulf Coast of the US. Storm: University of Wisconsin, Madison Cooperative Institute for Meteorogical Satellite Studies, 2005. Composite: Jack Gondela.

What are these emerging universals? What is new in basic design? Consider, for example, transparency—a concept explored in this book. Transparency is a condition in which two or more surfaces or substances are visible through each other. We constantly experience transparency in the physical environment: from water, glass, and smoke to venetian blinds, slatted fences, and perforated screens. Graphic designers across the modern period have worked with transparency, but never more so than today, when transparency can be instantly manipulated with commonly used tools.

What does transparency *mean*? Transparency can be used to construct thematic relationships. For example, compressing two pictures into a single space can suggest a conflict or synthesis of ideas (East/West, male/female, old/new). Designers also employ transparency as a compositional (rather than thematic) device, using it to soften edges, establish emphasis, separate competing elements, and so on.

Transparency is crucial to the vocabulary of film and motion-based media. In place of a straight cut, an animator or editor diminishes the opacity of an image over time (fade to black) or mixes two semitransparent images (cross dissolve). Such transitions affect a film's rhythm and style. They also modulate, in subtle ways, the message or content of the work. Although viewers rarely stop to interpret these transitions, a video editor or animator understands them as part of the basic language of moving images.

Layering is another universal concept with rising importance. Physical printing processes use layers (ink on paper), and so do software interfaces (from layered Photoshop files to sound or motion timelines).

Transparency and layering have always been at play in the graphic arts. In today's context, what makes them new again is their omnipresent accessibility through software. Powerful digital tools are commonly available to professional artists and designers but also to children, amateurs, and tinkerers of every stripe. Their language has become universal.

Software tools provide models of visual media, but they don't tell us what to make or what to say. It is the designer's task to produce works that are relevant to living situations (audience, context, program, brief, site) and to deliver meaningful messages and rich, embodied experiences. Each producer animates design's core structures from his or her own place in the world.

Beyond the Basics

Jennifer Cole Phillips

Even the most robust visual language is useless without the ability to engage it in a living context. While this book centers around formal structure and experiment, some opening thoughts on process and problem solving are appropriate here, as we hope readers will reach not only for more accomplished form, but for form that resonates with fresh meaning.

Before the Macintosh, solving graphic design problems meant outsourcing at nearly every stage of the way: manuscripts were sent to a typesetter; photographs—selected from contact sheets—were printed at a lab and corrected by a retoucher; and finished artwork was the job of a paste-up artist, who sliced and cemented type and images onto boards. This protocol slowed down the work process and required designers to plan each step methodically.

By contrast, easily accessed software, cloud storage, ubiquitous wi-fi, and powerful laptops now allow designers and users to control and create complex work flows from almost anywhere.

Yet, as these digital technologies afford greater freedom and convenience, they also require ongoing education and upkeep. This recurring learning curve, added to already overloaded schedules, often cuts short the creative window for concept development and formal experimentation.

In the college context, students arrive ever more digitally adept. Acculturated by social media, smart phones, iPads, and apps, design students command the technical savvy that used to take years to build. This network know-how, though, does not necessarily translate into creative thinking.

Too often, the temptation to turn directly to the computer precludes deeper levels of research and ideation—the distillation zone that unfolds beyond the average appetite for testing the waters and exploring alternatives. People, places, thoughts, and things become familiar through repeated exposure. It stands to reason, then, that initial ideas and, typically, the top tiers of a Google search turn up only cursory results that are often tired and trite.

Getting to more interesting territory requires the perseverance to sift, sort, and assimilate subjects and solutions until a fresh spark emerges and takes hold.

Visual Thinking Ubiquitous access to image editing and design software, together with zealous media inculcation on all things design, has created a tidal wave of design makers outside the profession. Indeed, in our previous book, *D.I.Y.: Design It Yourself*, we extolled the virtues of learning and making, arguing that people acquire pleasure, knowledge, and power by engaging with design at all levels.

This volume shifts the climate of the conversation. Instead of skimming the surface, we dig deeper. Rather than issuing instructions, we frame problems and suggest possibilities. Inside, you will find many examples, by students and professionals, that balance and blend idiosyncrasy with formal discipline.

Rather than focus on practical problems such as how to design a book, brochure, app, or website, this book encourages readers to experiment with the visual language of design. By "experiment," we mean the process of examining a form, material, or process in a methodical yet open-ended way. To experiment is to isolate elements of an operation, limiting some variables in order to better study others. An experiment asks a question or tests a hypothesis whose answer is not known in advance.

Choose your corner, pick away at it carefully, intensely and to the best of your ability and that way **you might change the world.** Charles Eames

The book is organized around some of the formal elements and phenomena of design. In practice, those components mix and overlap, as they do in the examples shown throughout the book. By focusing attention on particular aspects of visual form, we encourage readers to recognize the forces at play behind strong graphic solutions. Likewise, while a dictionary presents specific words in isolation, those words come alive in the active context of writing and speaking.

Filtered through formal and conceptual experimentation, design thinking fuses a shared discipline with organic interpretation.

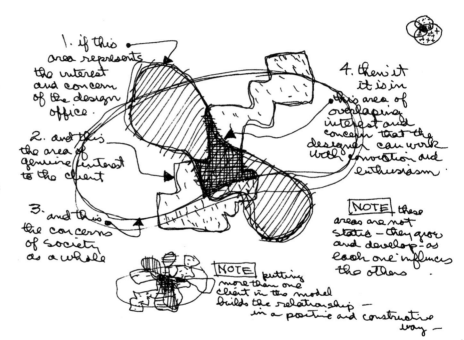

Diagramming Process Charles Eames drew this diagram to explain the design process as achieving a point where the needs and interests of the client, the designer, and society as a whole overlap. Charles Eames, 1969, for the exhibition *What is Design* at the Musée des Arts décoratifs, Paris, France. © 2007 Eames Office LLC.

Formstorming

I like a lot the adage that for every problem there is a solution that is simple, obvious, and wrong. **A problem worthy of the name is seldom accessible to sudden and simple solution.** Malcolm Grear

In a world where almost every designer has instant access to vast image databases and online search sites, there is little wonder why the landscape of contemporary graphic design is mired in mediocre solutions that capitalize on convenience. Many designers are not familiar with the kind of rigorous processes that might lead to higher levels of formal and conceptual innovation.

Formstorming is an act of visual thinking—a tool for designers to unlock and deepen solutions to basic design problems. This chapter presents several formstorming exercises designed to trigger and tease out options and ideas that go beyond the familiar, prompting designers to find fresh ways to illuminate subjects through guided creative engagement.

Formstorming moves the maker through automatic, easily conceived notions, toward recognizable yet nuanced concepts, to surprising results that compel us with their originality. The endurance required to stick with a subject through exhaustive iteration, dissection, synthesis, revision, and representation takes discipline and drive, but this level of immersion yields an unexpected and profound return on the creative investment.

In design school students are cautioned against turning too quickly to the computer, eclipsing the ideation phase. Still, many designers engage the process of concept generation thinly, soon landing in a place that seems promising and then starting prematurely to build out that idea. The result of such a truncated development phase is dull design that, at best, seems slick and eye-catching and, at worst, appears instantly dispensable.

Top chefs remind us that a great dish depends on top-notch ingredients. Likewise, in graphic design, we must strive for excellence in each part of our design. The principles and processes demonstrated in this chapter may be used to elevate and extend any of the design basics covered in this book and beyond.

In a complex world that is filtered through layers of visual, verbal, and sensory signals, robust, clear visual communication is key. Excellent design not only helps us make sense of our lives, but it can make the experience a pleasurable one.

Photo Constructions Designer Martin Venezky made this image of reconstructed details from a large collage wall he generated in a three-day formstorming exercise for *All Possible Futures*, an exhibition by Jon Sueda. Martin Venezky, Appetite Engineers.

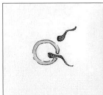

One Hundred Iterations

Generating multiple iterations of one subject is a means of digging deeper. By repeatedly tapping into our mental database of associations and ideas, we are able to exhaust the obvious and get to fresher territory. This classic exercise asks designers to choose one subject and visually interpret it in one hundred ways. Basic semiotic principles—the icon, index, and symbol—are introduced to expand the scope of thinking and representation. Students make, capture, and appropriate imagery that, as a collection, has depth and breadth conceptually and formally, with an emphasis on excellence and innovation. MFA Studio. Jennifer Cole Phillips, faculty.

 One dozen.

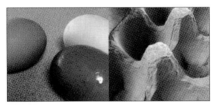

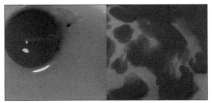

Don't put all your eggs in one basket.

Dozens of Eggs This designer chose a bound book to house her one hundred egg iterations. Basic semiotic modes of representation helped probe the subject from multiple angles. *Indexical signs*, such as the nest, shell, sperm, and carton, point to the subject, while *icons*, such as photographs and illustrations of eggs, resemble the subject. *Symbols*, such as a Humpty Dumpty, rely on shared cultural understanding. Multipage formats challenge the designer to address a layer of pacing and parallelism. Jackie Littman.

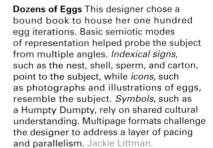 Benedict.

 Hard boiled.

A Plus Working with the letter A, the designer found or created one hundred diverse and graphically compelling images. She arranged the edited collection inside and around a gridded template, paying careful attention to the distribution of color, texture, depth of field, and gesture in order to engage the viewer's eye throughout the composition. Yingxi Zhou.

Colleen Roxas

Formstorming Templates

These templates can serve as inspiring vessels to capture, collect, and curate evolving visual and verbal ideas related to projects. Designers use formatted templates to mindfully conduct essential investigations, such as research precedents, engage in visual thinking, draft sketches, and explore various visual and verbal voices, vehicles, component formats, and media and materials. A multi-column grid helps distribute and arrange subject matter, and captions and context summaries reference and record design thinking. Advanced Graphic Design II and MFA Studio. Jennifer Cole Phillips, faculty.

Beyond the Sketchbook Selecting, synthesizing, rendering, representing, and installing visual ideas into templates provides an added layer of clarity and curation, and serves as a more professional process record than a sketchbook. Aura Selzer.

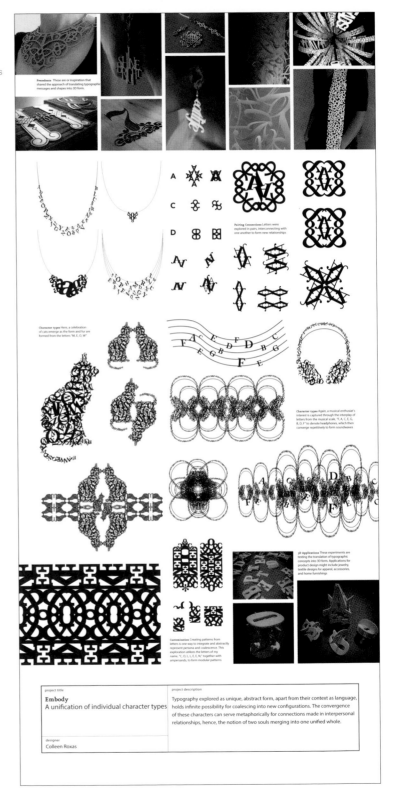

project title	project description
Embody A unification of individual character types	Typography explored as unique, abstract form, apart from their context as language, holds infinite possibility for coalescing into new configurations. The convergence of these characters can serve metaphorically for connections made in interpersonal relationships, hence, the notion of two souls merging into one unified whole.
designer Colleen Roxas	

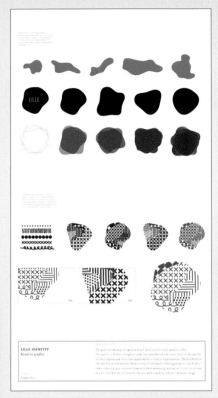

Jasper Crocker

Yingxi Zhou

Julian Haddad

Design Investigation Undergraduate seniors at MICA are required to frame and solve a semester-long design investigation of their choosing. Often daunted by the open-ended nature of this challenge, they turn to formstorming templates, which help them organize and deepen their work.

Breaking the Block This designer collected
strategies for getting beyond creative blocks
and translated them into experimental
typographic form that fell outside his own
comfort zone. Brian Pelsoh, MFA Studio.

Trending Hashtags This designer chose a daily trending Twitter hashtag as fodder for dimensional typographic experiments. Amanda Buck, MFA Studio.

Dailies

This ongoing generative exercise spurs design thinking through a daily creative act situated within a conceptual framework. Designers are prompted to define the parameters of the daily act, including the conceptual framework, medium, and format. The rigor and momentum involved in creating a design-a-day help students build key discipline and time management skills and yield a robust body of work that develops the designer's portfolio and process. Dailies generally span at least two weeks and sometimes involve creating a container or system to house the work and add context. MFA Studio. Jennifer Cole Phillips, faculty.

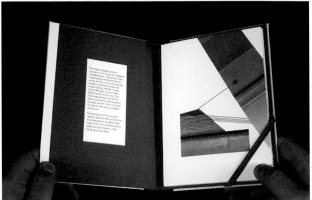

Daily Collage Project These collaged compositions were inspired by hand sketches of famous modern architects, such as Frank Gehry, Zaha Hadid, and Frank Lloyd Wright. A controlled color palette and consistent visual vocabulary insure cohesiveness across a wide range of experimental form.
Jessica Wen, Advanced Graphic Design I.
Jennifer Cole Phillips, faculty.

Happier. Feeling down? Getting anxious? We've got something for you. Just plug in the patented happi-stick to your device's headphone jack and stick your finger in. We'll give you a tiny prick, test your blood for chemical imbalances, then have a pharmacist deliver the right prescription to your door. Feeling good has never been easier.

Instagramaphone. Show off your love for vintage music with Instagramaphone, the hot new audio filter. Why should everything sound so clean? With Instagramaphone, you can add audio filters like "vinyl" and "AM radio" to create authentic background noise from a simpler era. Create playlists from iTunes, Spotify, Rdio, and more to play your favorite songs with a nostalgic twist.

Happier			Progeny
Pixl8r			HealthNut
Instagramophone			FeedMe
MidasTouch			Uninterrupt
iPoo			MEmoji
Liar, Liar			Presence
Brain2Text			MatchMaker

App a Day This student created fourteen fictitious apps in fourteen days as an exercise in rapid design. The apps form a dystopic family that lampoons society and blurs the lines of what is possible, what is legal, and what is worthwhile. Emma Sherwood-Forbes, MFA Studio.

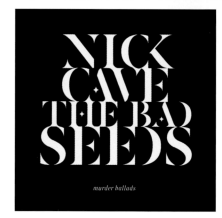

Record a Day Passionate about music, this designer challenged himself to match the musical moxy and tenor of a collection of his favorite albums, using color, composition, and custom typography on a series of daily LP cover designs. Shiva Nallaperumal, MFA Studio.

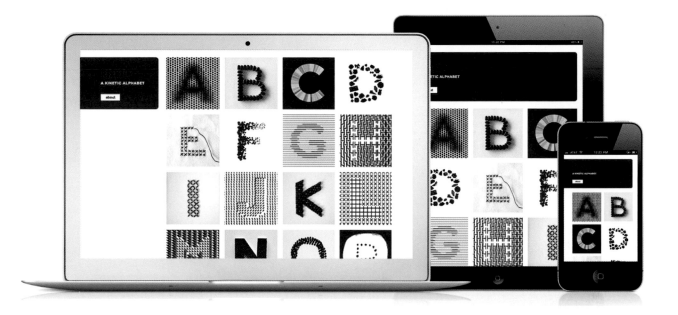

Daily Movements For this project the designer created an animated series of two- and three-dimensional letterform experiments built from a variety of digital and analog bits over the course of a month, and then built a website to showcase the alphabet on screen. Jackie Littman, MFA Studio.

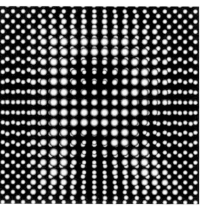

Process Verbs After building a solid typographic composition, designers applied a series of actions (both physical and digital) to their initial design. The actions were prompted by a list of verbs, including *fold, cut, tear, touch, warp, reflect, multiply, copy, disperse, compress,* and *reflect*. Each designer chose how to turn these verbs into design processes and outcomes. Typography II. Ellen Lupton, faculty.

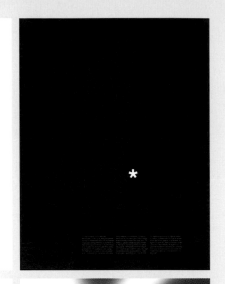

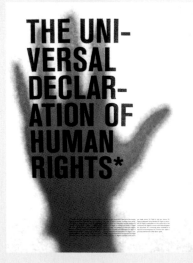

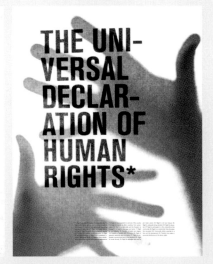

Nick Fogarty

Laura
Brewer-Yarnall

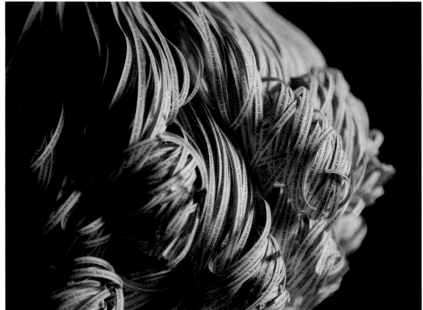

Alterego: Literary Stylist This literature-obsessed hairstylist pays tribute to his favorite authors by surgically slicing lines of their prose into strands of hair and fashioning them into hairstyles reflective of the work's era and affect. In the exhibition space, an expertly crafted film capturing the coiffing plays in the background. Chen Yu.

Alterego

This project invites each designer
to develop a fictitious persona that
amplifies, undermines,or rediscovers
an element of themselves and
then to design through the lens
of that character. Alterego pushes
designers to step outside and
beyond their comfort zone and
experiment with fresh design
language, media, and making. At
MICA, the project culminates in
an exhibition where students bring
their character to life in a three-
dimensional setting. MFA Studio.
Silas Munro and Jennifer Cole
Phillips, faculty.

Alterego: Fashion Sense This alterego is an
internationally renowned fashion designer
with a penchant for sleek silhouettes, taut
asymmetry, and bold graphic form, texture,
and tonality. Yingxi Zhou.

Alterego: After Hours The persona here is
an elite madam at the helm of an exclusive
"escort service." Once clients are thoroughly
screened, they receive this provocative
black box containing only a card with a web
address. The site has no information other
than a seductive motion graphic designed to
attract new business. Jamie Carusi.

Alterego: Identity Disorder The alterego is a German psychiatrist specializing in multiple and dissociative identity disorders. Through multiple-exposure photography meticulously stitched together, he captures and fuses fractured persona parts into one cohesive whole, creating a sort of snapshot of the psychosis. David Dale.

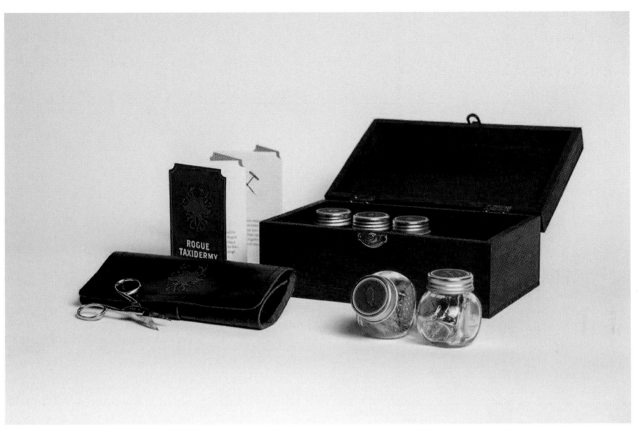

Alterego: Rogue Taxidermist Odds & Ends
for the Rogue Taxidermist is a concept design
for a taxidermist's toolkit. Wood, leather,
glass, metal, and paper were carefully crafted
to create a credible visual vernacular.
Jackie Littman.

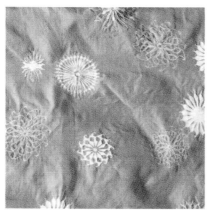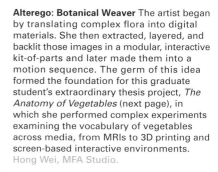

Alterego: Botanical Weaver The artist began by translating complex flora into digital materials. She then extracted, layered, and backlit those images in a modular, interactive kit-of-parts and later made them into a motion sequence. The germ of this idea formed the foundation for this graduate student's extraordinary thesis project, *The Anatomy of Vegetables* (next page), in which she performed complex experiments examining the vocabulary of vegetables across media, from MRIs to 3D printing and screen-based interactive environments. Hong Wei, MFA Studio.

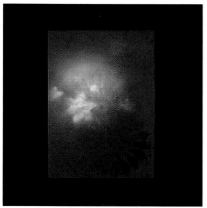

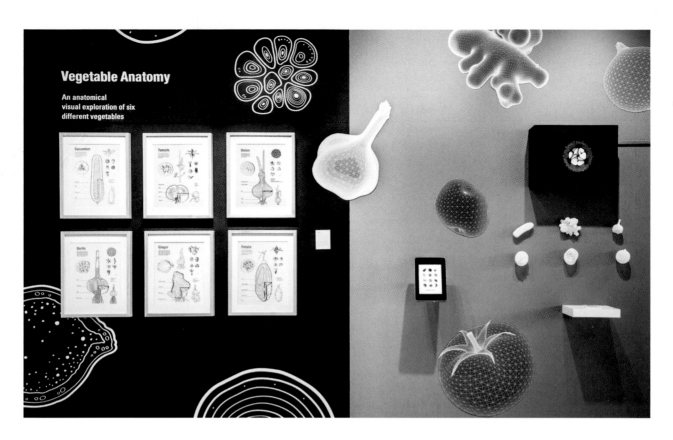

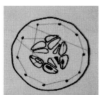

Thesis: Vegetable Anatomy The alterego project (left page) ignited this designer's appetite for rigorous and elaborate experimentation with complex and multiple media. Her thesis project, *The Anatomy of Vegetables*, starts with material studies, dissection, and analysis, which are then transformed into tangible contexts, such as a highly interactive app, grocery tote bags, animations, and a website. The clearly articulated hierarchy, and sleek, distilled thesis exhibition design (above) belie the thousands of generative investigations the designer performed throughout the process. Hong Wei, MFA Studio.

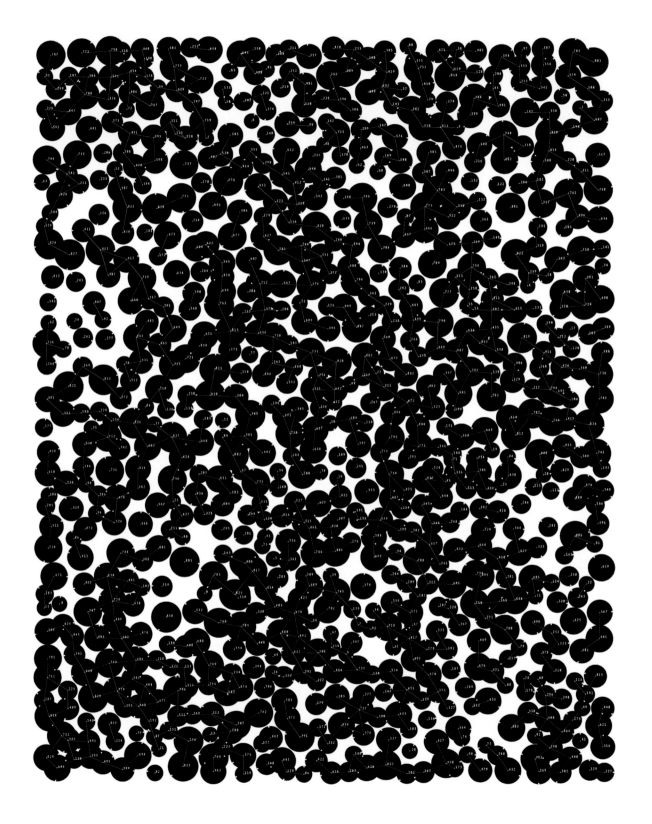

A line is the track made by the moving point…

It is created by movement—specifically through the destruction of the intense, self-contained repose of the point. Wassily Kandinsky

Id	0	1	2	3
X	224.543	715.448	227.491	313.495
Y	247.001	879.651	839.485	291.144
Size	20.000	20.024	20.048	20.072
Angle	1.429	1.000	4.141	0.144
Others	2	1	2	1
	29	30	31	32	33
	396.477	386.946	655.302	347.761	158.650
	396.899	468.870	242.406	625.749	466.553
	20.691	20.715	20.739	20.763	20.787
	4.687	5.715	5.395	3.691	6.245
	1	3	2	2	2
	59	60	61	62	63
	388.065	450.679	302.301	18.621	9.702
	269.422	795.973	319.802	598.880	782.143
	21.406	21.430	21.454	21.478	21.502
	2.471	2.117	1.626	0.988	3.603
	1	1	2	1	2
	89	90	91	92	93
	247.620	67.441	13.802	90.058	440.551
	450.361	388.695	920.408	602.967	200.302
	22.122	22.145	22.169	22.193	22.217
	2.354	0.952	2.805	0.112	2.384
	4	3	2	1	2

Point to Line Processing is a programming language created by C. E. B. Reas and Benjamin Fry. In this digital drawing by Reas, the lines express a relationship among the points, derived from numerical data. C. E. B. Reas, *Process 4 (Form/Data 1)*, 2005 (detail).

Point, line, and plane are the building blocks of design. From these elements, designers create images, icons, textures, patterns, diagrams, animations, and typographic systems. Indeed, every complex design shown in this book results at some level from the interaction of points, lines, and planes.

Diagrams build relationships among elements using points, lines, and planes to map and connect data. Textures and patterns are constructed from large groups of points and lines that repeat, rotate, and otherwise interact to form distinctive and engaging surfaces. Typography consists of individual letters (points) that form into lines and fields of text.

For hundreds of years, printing processes have employed dots and lines to depict light, shadow, and volume. Different printing technologies support distinct kinds of mark making. To produce a woodcut, for example, the artist carves out material from a flat surface. In contrast to this subtractive process, lithography allows the artist to make positive, additive marks across a surface. In these processes, dots and lines accumulate to build larger planes and convey the illusion of volume.

Photography, invented in the early 1800s, captures reflected light automatically. The subtle tonal variations of photography eliminated the intermediary mesh of point and line.

Yet reproducing the tones of a photographic image requires translating it into pure graphic marks, because nearly every mechanical printing method—from lithography to laser printing—works with solid inks. The halftone process, invented in the 1880s and still used today, converts a photograph into a pattern of larger and smaller dots, simulating tonal variation with pure spots of black or flat color. The same principle is used in digital reproduction.

Today, designers use software to capture the gestures of the hand as data that can be endlessly manipulated and refined. Software describes images in terms of point, line, plane, shape, and volume as well as color, transparency, and other features. There are numerous ways to experiment with these basic elements of two-dimensional design: observing the environment around you, making marks with physical and digital tools, using software to create and manipulate images, or writing code to generate form with rules and variables.

x = 4.5521 in
y = 0.997 in

Point

A point marks a position in space.
In pure geometric terms, a point is
a pair of x, y coordinates. It has
no mass at all. Graphically, however,
a point takes form as a dot, a visible
mark. A point can be an insignificant
fleck of matter or a concentrated
locus of power. It can penetrate like
a bullet, pierce like a nail, or
pucker like a kiss. Through its scale,
position, and relationship to its
surroundings, a point can express its
own identity or melt into the crowd.

A series of points forms a line.
A mass of points becomes texture,
shape, or plane. Tiny points of
varying size create shades of gray.

The tip of an arrow points
the way, just as the crossing of an X
marks a spot.

In typography, the point is a
period—the definitive end of a line.
Each character in a field of text is a
singular element, and thus a kind of
point, a finite element in a series.

end of a line.

In typography, each character
in a field of text is a point, a
finite element represented
by a single key stroke. The
letter occupies a position in a
larger line or plane of text. At
the end of the line is a period.
The point is a sign of closure,
of finality. It marks the end.

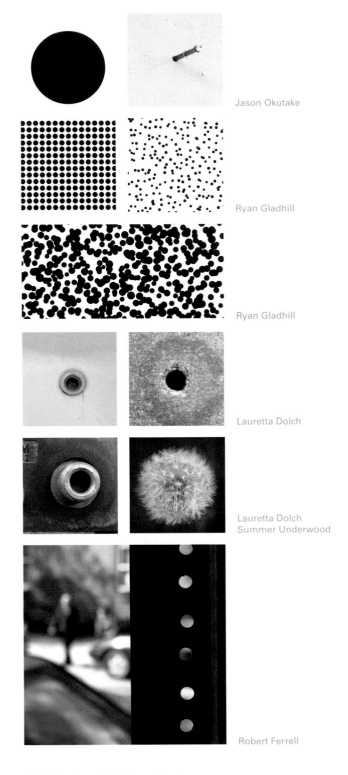

Jason Okutake

Ryan Gladhill

Ryan Gladhill

Lauretta Dolch

Lauretta Dolch
Summer Underwood

Robert Ferrell

Digital Imaging. Al Maskeroni, faculty.

Destructive Points Never underestimate the power of a point. This damaged facade was photographed in the war-torn city of Mostar, on the Balkan Peninsula in Bosnia and Herzegovina. Nancy Froehlich.

length = .9792 in

Jeremy Botts

Lines express emotions.

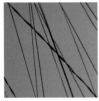

Josh Sims
Bryan McDonough

Alex Ebright
Justin Lloyd

Digital Imaging.
Nancy Froehlich,
faculty.

Lines describe structure and edges.

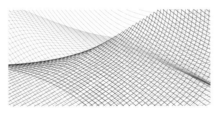

Allen Harrison

Lines turn and multiply to describe planes.

Line

A line is an infinite series of points. Understood geometrically, a line has length, but no breadth. A line is the connection between two points, or it is the path of a moving point.

A line can be a positive mark or a negative gap. Lines appear at the edges of objects and where two planes meet.

Graphically, lines exist in many weights; the thickness and texture as well as the path of the mark determine its visual presence. Lines are drawn with a pen, pencil, brush, mouse, or digital code. They can be straight or curved, continuous or broken. When a line reaches a certain thickness, it becomes a plane. Lines multiply to describe volumes, planes, and textures.

A graph is a rising and falling line that describes change over time, as in a waveform charting a heart beat or an audio signal.

In typographic layouts, lines are implied as well as literally drawn. Characters group into lines of text, while columns are positioned in blocks that are flush left, flush right, and justified. Imaginary lines appear along the edges of each column, expressing the order of the page.

Type sits on a baseline.

Typographic alignment refers to the organization of text into columns with a hard or soft edge. A justified column is even along both the left and right sides.

The crisp edge of a column is implied by the even starting or ending points of successive lines of type. The eye connects the points to make a line. Such typographic lines are implied, not drawn.

Line/Shape Study Vector-based software
uses a closed line to define a shape. Here,
new lines are formed by the intersection of
shapes, creating a swelling form reminiscent
of the path of a steel-point pen. Ryan
Gladhill, MFA Studio.

width = 0.9792 in
height = 0.9792 in

Plane

A plane is a flat surface extending in height and width. A plane is the path of a moving line; it is a line with breadth. A line closes to become a shape, a bounded plane. Shapes are planes with edges. In vector-based software, every shape consists of line and fill. A plane can be parallel to the picture surface, or it can skew and recede into space. Ceilings, walls, floors, and windows are physical planes. A plane can be solid or perforated, opaque or transparent, textured or smooth.

A field of text is a plane built from points and lines of type. A typographic plane can be dense or open, hard or soft. Designers experiment with line spacing, font size, and alignment to create different typographic shapes.

In typography, letters gather into lines, and lines build up into planes. The quality of the plane—its density or opacity, its heaviness or lightness on the page—is determined by the size of the letters, the spacing between lines, words, and characters, and the visual character of a given typeface.

In typography, letters gather into lines, and lines build up into planes. The quality of the plane—its density, its opacity, its weight on the page—is determined by the size of the letters, the spacing between lines, words, and characters, and the visual character of a given typeface.

Hard, closed shape

Soft, open shape

Plane Letters A plane can be described with lines or with fields of color. These letterforms use ribbons of color to describe spatial planes. Kelly Horigan, Experimental Typography. Ken Barber, faculty.

**Parallel Lines
Converge**
Summer
Underwood

Space and Volume

A graphic object that encloses three-dimensional space has volume. It has height, width, and depth. A sheet of paper or a computer screen has no real depth, of course, so volume is represented through graphic conventions.

Linear perspective simulates optical distortions, making near objects appear large as far objects become small, receding into nothing as they reach the horizon. The angle at which elements recede reflects the position of the viewer. Are the objects above or below the viewer's eye level? Camera lenses replicate the effects of linear perspective, recording the position of the camera's eye.

Axonometric projections depict volume without making elements recede into space. The scale of elements thus remains consistent as objects move back into space. The result is more abstract and impersonal than linear perspective.

Architects often use axono-metric projections in order to keep a consistent scale across the page. Digital game designers often use this technique as well, creating maps of simulated worlds rather than depicting experience from the ground.

Projection Study This idealized landscape uses axonometric projection, in which scale is consistent from the front to back of the image. As seen on a map or computer game, this space implies a disembodied, godlike viewer rather than a physical eye positioned in relation to a horizon. Visakh Menon, MFA Studio.

Yeohyun Ahn

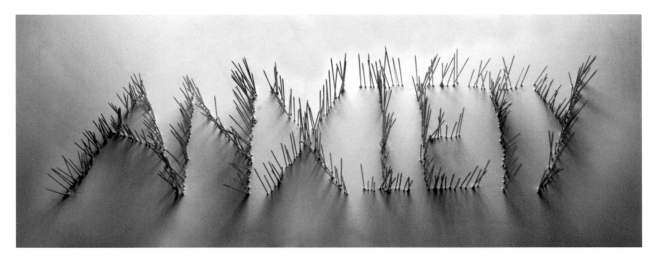

Visakh Menon

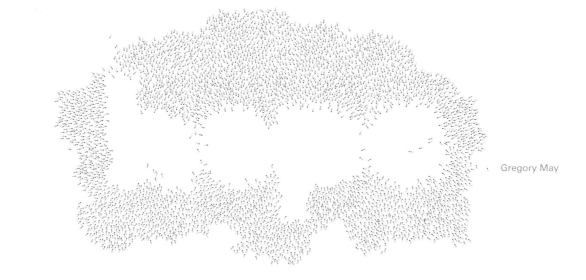

Gregory May

Yeohyun Ahn

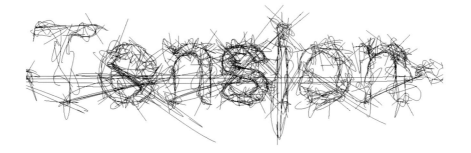

Jason Okutake

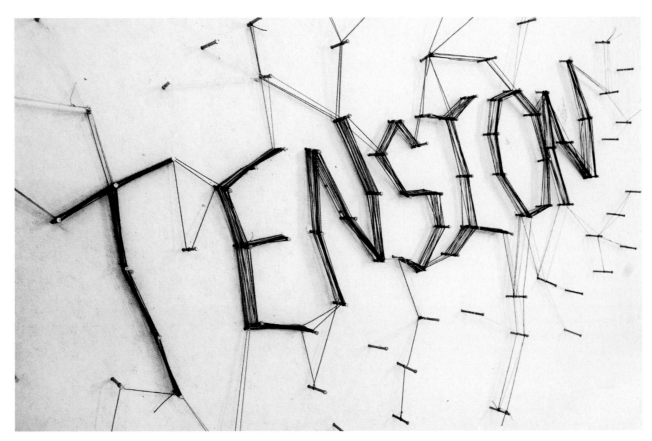

Point and Line: Physical and Digital In the lettering experiments shown here, each word is written with lines, points, or both, produced with physical elements, digital illustrations, or code-generated vectors. MFA Studio. Marian Bantjes, visiting faculty.

Three Objects, Thirty-Three Ways

This comprehensive design project encourages designers to observe, represent, and abstract visible objects using a variety of materials and techniques. Designers begin by visiting an unusual place with surprising things to see and observe, such as a local museum, aquarium, or botanical garden. They produce a substantial number of observational drawings of three objects, paying special attention to the appearance of form, color, texture, and materials. Careful observation is followed by exercises in creating word lists and drawing from memory to create a total of ninety-nine studies. The project exposes designers to the iterative design process, building individual capacity for patience, endurance, and an open mind.

Graphic Design I. Brockett Horne, faculty.

Trevor Carr

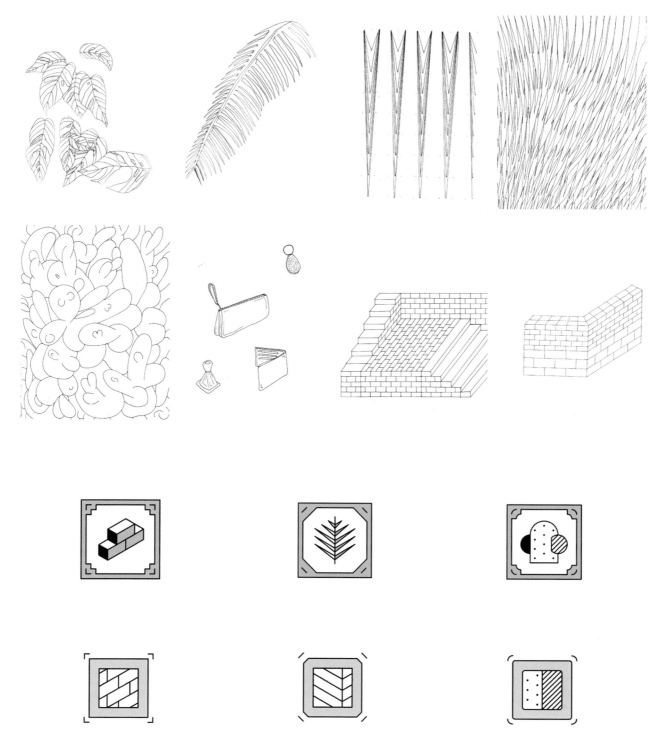

Michael Quednau

Jen Evans

Spatial Translation

In this project, designers explore point, line, and plane as tools for expression. They immerse themselves in a space and observe it from multiple points of view, including different vantage points (above, below) and different psychological orientations (as a male, a female, a giraffe, a shrimp, etc.). Participants generate images of their chosen spaces in diverse media, including photography, drawing, painting, printing, collage, or video. Representations can be literal, abstract, iconic, indexical, or symbolic. After gathering their initial observations, designers create a series of representations using dot stickers, tape, and cut paper. The final application is a sequence of ten images suitable for an accordion fold book. Graphic Design I. Brockett Horne, faculty.

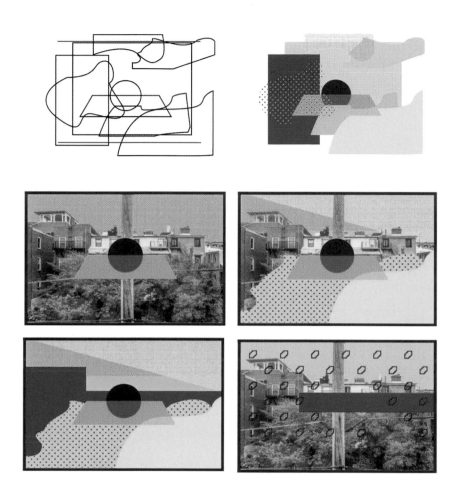

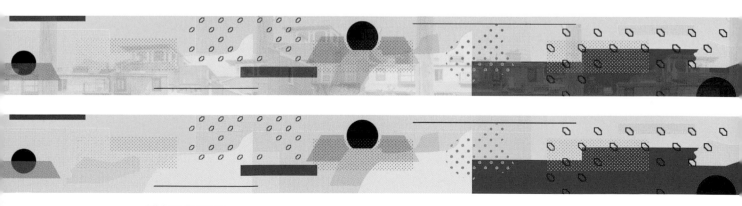

Michael Quednau

BinaryTree(400,600,400,550,30,1);

BinaryTree(400,600,400,550,30,3);

Drawing with Code

The drawings shown here were created with Processing, an open-source software application. The designs are built from a binary tree, a basic data structure in which each node spawns at most two offspring. Binary trees are used to organize information hierarchies, and they often take a graphical form. The density of the final drawing depends on the angle between the "children" and the number of generations.

The larger design is created by repeating, rotating, inverting, connecting, and overlapping the tree forms. In code-based drawing, the designer varies the results by changing the inputs to the algorithm.

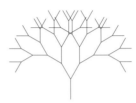

BinaryTree(400,600,400,550,30,5);

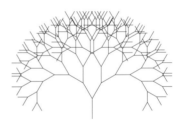

BinaryTree(400,600,400,550,30,7);

BinaryTree(400,600,400,550,30,9);

Binary Tree The drawing becomes denser with each generation. The last number in the code indicates the number of iterations. Yeohyun Ahn, MFA Studio.

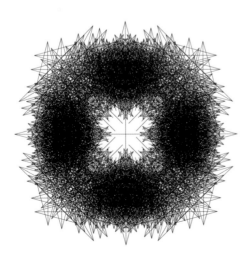

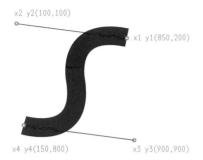

x2 y2(100,100)
x1 y1(850,200)
x4 y4(150,800)
x3 y3(900,900)

```
bezier(850,200,100,100,900,900,150,800);
```

```
for(int i=0; i<900; i=i+100)
{bezier(850,200,100,100,i,900,150,800);}
```

Bézier Curves

A Bézier curve is a line defined by a set of anchor and control points. Designers are accustomed to drawing curves using vector-based software and then modifying the curve by adding, subtracting, and repositioning the anchor and control points.

The drawings shown here were created with the open-source software application Processing. The curves were drawn directly in code:

```
bezier(x1,y1,x2,y2,x3,y3,x4,y4);
```

The first two parameters (x1, y1) specify the first anchor point, and the last two parameters (x4, y4) specify the other anchor point. The middle parameters locate the control points that define the curve.

Curves drawn with standard illustration software are fundamentally the same as curves drawn in code, but we understand and control them with different means. The designer varies the results by changing the inputs to the algorithm.

```
for(int i=0;i<900; i=i+40)
{bezier(i,200,100,100,900,i,150,800);}
```

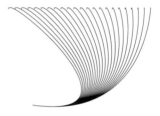

```
for(int i=0;i<900;i=i+40)
{bezier(i,200,i,100,900,900,150,800);}
```

Repeated Bézier Curve The designer has written a function that repeats the curve in space according to a given increment (i). The same basic code was used to generate all the drawings shown above, with varied inputs for the anchor and control points. A variable (i) defines the curve. Yeohyun Ahn, MFA Studio.

```
beginShape(POLYGON);
vertex(30,20);
bezierVertex(80,0,80,75,30,75);
bezierVertex(50,80,60,25,30,20);
endShape()
```

Black Flower A Bézier vertex is a shape created by closing a Bézier curve. This design was created by rotating numerous Bézier vertices around a common center, with varying degrees of transparency. Yeohyun Ahn, MFA Studio.

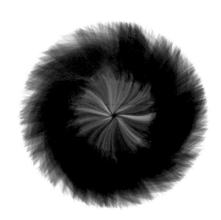

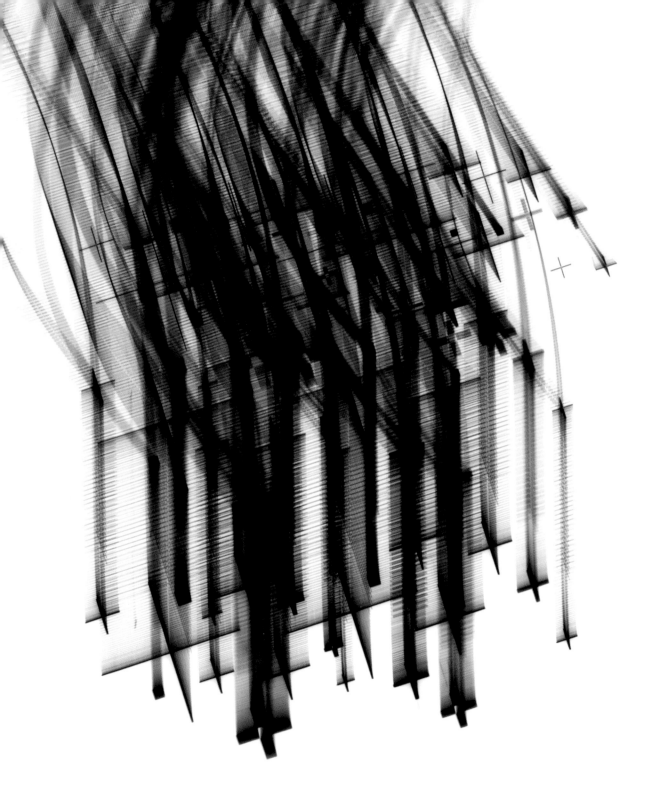

I pay close attention to the variety of shapes and sizes, and place the objects so that **the lines and edges create a rhythm** that guides the viewer's eye around the image and into the focal point.

Sergei Forostovskii

Rhythm and Repetition This code-driven photogram employs a simple stencil plus sign through which light is projected as the photo paper shifts minutely and mechanically across the span of hours. The visual result has the densely layered richness of a charcoal drawing. Tad Takano. Photographed for reproduction by Dan Meyers.

Balance is a fundamental human condition: we require physical balance to stand upright and walk; we seek balance among the many facets of our personal and professional lives; the world struggles for balance of power. Indeed, balance is a prized commodity in our culture, and it is no surprise that our implicit, intuitive relationship with it has equipped us to sense balance—or imbalance— in the things we see, hear, smell, taste, and touch.

In design, balance acts as a catalyst for form—it anchors and activates elements in space. Do you ever notice your eye getting stuck in a particular place when looking at an unresolved design? This discord usually occurs because the proportion and placement of elements in relation to each other and to the negative space is off—too big, too tight, too flat, misaligned, and so on.

Relationships among elements on the page remind us of physical relationships. Visual balance occurs when the weight of one or more things is distributed evenly or proportionately in space. Like arranging furniture in a room, we move components around until the balance of form and space feels just right. Large objects are a counterpoint to smaller ones; dark objects to lighter ones.

A symmetrical design, which has the same elements on at least two sides along a common axis, is inherently stable. Yet balance need not be static. A tightrope walker achieves balance while traversing a precarious line in space, continually shifting her weight while staying in constant motion. Designers employ contrasting size, texture, value, color, and shape to offset or emphasize the weight of an object and achieve the acrobat's dynamic sense of balance.

Rhythm is a strong, regular, repeated pattern: the beating of drums, the patter of rain, the falling of footsteps. Speech, music, and dance all employ rhythm to express form over time. Graphic designers use rhythm in the construction of static images as well as in books, magazines, and motion graphics that have duration and sequence. Although pattern design usually employs unbroken repetition, most forms of graphic design seek rhythms that are punctuated with change and variation. Book design, for example, seeks out a variety of scales and tonal values across its pages, while also preserving an underlying structural unity.

Balance and rhythm work together to create works of design that pulse with life, achieving both stability and surprise.

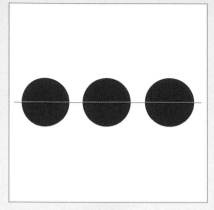

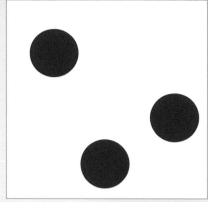

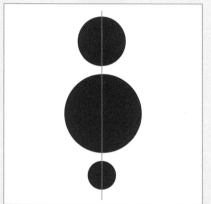

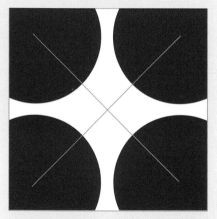

Symmetry and Asymmetry

Symmetry can be left to right, top to bottom, or both. Many natural organisms have a symmetrical form. The even weighting of arms and legs helps insure a creature's safe mobility; a tree develops an even distribution of weight around its core to stand erect; and the arms of a starfish radiate from the center.

Symmetry is not the only way to achieve balance, however. Asymmetrical designs are generally more active than symmetrical ones, and designers achieve balance by placing contrasting elements in counterpoint to each other, yielding compositions that allow the eye to wander while achieving an overall stability.

Symmetry The studies above demonstrate basic symmetrical balance. Elements are oriented along a common axis; the image mirrors from side to side along that axis. The configurations shown here are symmetrical from left to right and/or from top to bottom.

Asymmetry These studies use asymmetry to achieve compositional balance. Elements are placed organically, relying on the interaction of form and negative space and the proximity of elements to each other and to the edges of the field, yielding both tension and balance.

UGANDA IS WAVERING IN ITS FIGHT AGAINST HIV AIDS AS THE COUNTRY HAS WON INTERNATIONAL ACCLAIM FOR ITS PROGRESS AGAINST HIV AIDS THE LATEST NUMBERS HOWEVER INDICATE THAT UGANDA IS NOW LOSING GROUND THE GOVERNMENT IS BOWING TO PRESSURE FROM FAITH-BASED ORGANIZATIONS IN THE USA PUSHING RIGID MORALISTIC APPROACHES SUCH AS ABSTINENCE AND BEING FAITHFUL AT THE EXPENSE OF SAFER SEX PRACTICES THE FUNDAMENTAL ISSUE THE USE OF CONDOMS IS BEING IGNORED OR LEFT OUT COMPLETELY THE BUSH ADMINISTRATIONS $1.2 BILLION FUNDING TO UGANDA IS NOW IN QUESTION AS RATES OF HIV OR ARE RISING IT SEEMS AS THE HIV AND AIDS ABC CAMPAIGN HAS LOST ITS POWER CONDOMS ARE AN IMPROVISATION NOT A SOLUTION I FAVOR OPTIMAL RELATIONSHIPS BASED ON LOVE AND TRUST INSTEAD OF INTENTIONAL MISTRUST WHICH IS WHAT THE CONDOM IS ALL ABOUT CONDOMS HAVE BEEN BANNED BY THE GOVERNMENT OF UGANDA BECAUSE THEY PROMOTE SIGNIFICANT RISK TO THE POPULATION AT LARGE IT WAS FULFILLING WHAT THE GOVERNMENT HAD ORDERED A RECALL AND DESTRUCTION OF CONDOMS ABSTINENCE AND FIDELITY ARE THE MOST IMPORTANT FACTORS IN ENDING THE TRANSMISSION OF HIV PROGRAMS THAT RECEIVE PEPFAR FUNDS WILL NOT BE REQUIRED TO PROVIDE CONDOMS AS A MODE OF PREVENTION THE UNITED STATES ADMINISTRATION WILL TAKE ABSTINENCE FROM AN AFTERTHOUGHT FORWARD TO AN URGENT GOAL THE RELIGIOUS INSTITUTIONS ARE VITAL PARTICIPANTS IN THE FIGHT AGAINST HIV AND AIDS IN EVERY INSTANCE

Disrupted Symmetry The designer has disrupted this symmetrical cross form to signify political unrest among factions in Uganda around the HIV/AIDS crisis. Narrative text lines alternate between clarity and obfuscation, ultimately erupting in chaos, yielding a dynamic counterpoint balance. Katrina Keane, MFA Studio.

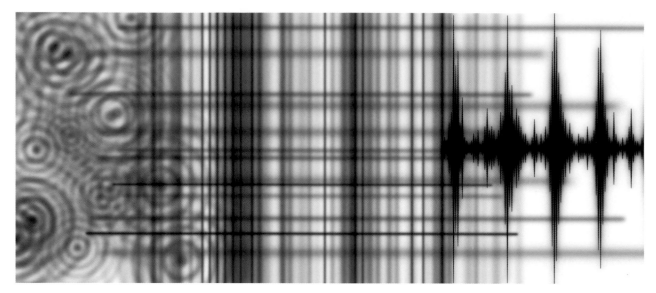

Jason Okutake, MFA Studio

Rhythm and Time

We are familiar with rhythm from the world of sound. In music, an underlying pattern changes in time. Layers of pattern occur simultaneously in music, supporting each other and providing aural contrast. In audio mixing, sounds are amplified or diminished to create a rhythm that shifts and evolves over the course of a piece.

Graphic designers employ similar structures visually. The repetition of elements such as circles, lines, and grids creates rhythm, while varying their size or intensity generates surprise. In animation, designers must orchestrate both audio and visual rhythms simultaneously.

Manic Mandala The smooth, symmetrical shapes layered to build this mandala are interrupted by a discordant frenzy of sharp, irregular lines and masses. Wenji Lu, MFA Studio.

Highway Overpasses, Houston, Texas

Repetition and Change

From the flowing contours of a farmer's fields to a sea of shipping containers stacked tightly into rows, repetition is an endless feature of the human environment. Like melodic consonance and fervent discord in music, repetition and change awaken life's visual juxtapositions. Beauty arises from the mix.

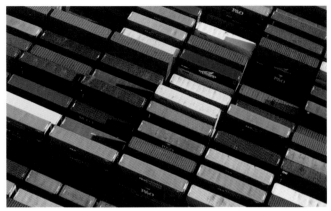

Shipping Containers, Norfolk, Virginia

Contour Farming, Meyersville, Maryland

Observed Rhythm Aerial photographs are fascinating and surprising because we are not accustomed to seeing landscapes from above. The many patterns, textures, and colors embedded in both man-made and natural forms—revealed and concealed through light and shadow—yield intriguing rhythms. Cameron Davidson.

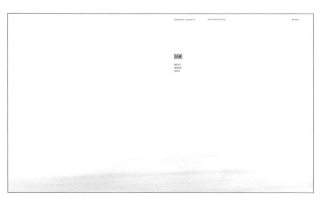
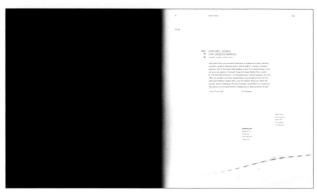
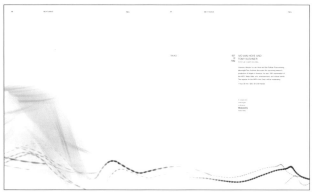

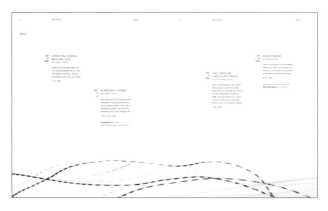
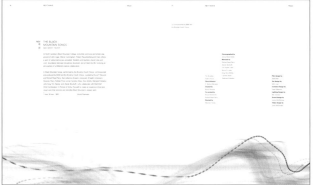

Rhythm and Pacing
Designers often work with content distributed across multiple pages. As in a single-page composition, 5an overall coherence. Imagery, typography, rules, color fields, and so on are placed with mindful intention to create focal points and to carry the viewer's eye through the piece. An underlying grid helps bring order to a progression of pages. Keeping an element of surprise and variation is key to sustaining interest.

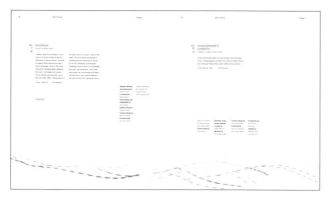

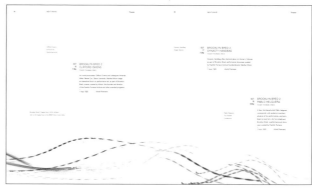

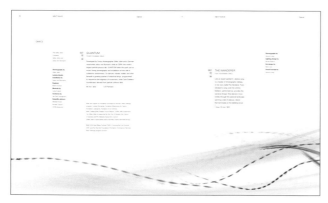

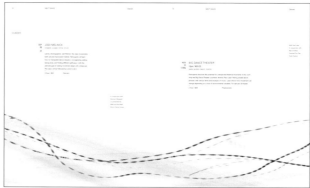

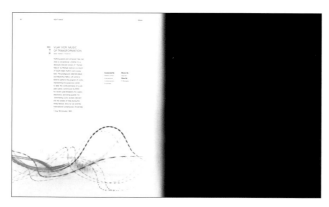

The Next Wave Festival This highly systematic project asks designers to create a program of events for the Brooklyn Academy of Music's Next Wave Festival. Given the sophisticated, avant-garde nature of the venue, designers are encouraged to reach for fresh solutions that will balance a spirit of invention and expression with navigable order and clearly accessible information.

This solution creates counterpoint contrast between the undulating and smoky wave forms and a rigorous grid system, hierarchy, and dynamic distribution within each spread and across the entire sequence.
Kim Meistrell, Advanced Graphic Design I.
Jennifer Cole Phillips, faculty.

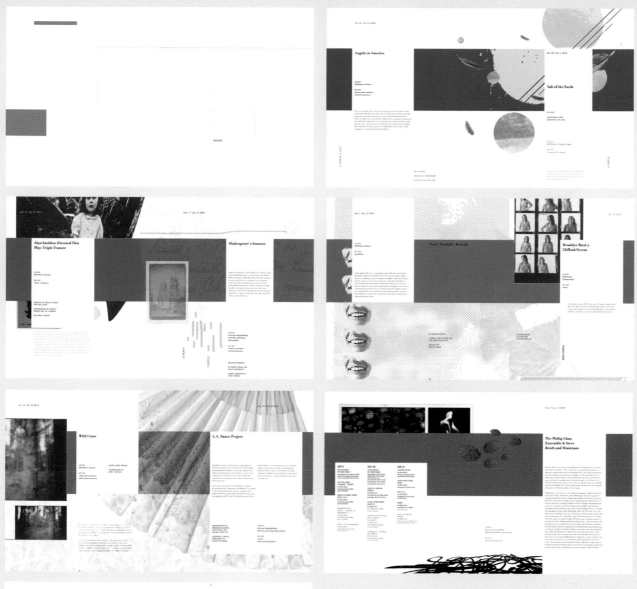

Ordered Improvisation The designer commands a complex and nuanced visual vocabulary, embedding a graceful balance of order and improvisation into compositions built with dynamic asymmetry across multiple spreads. Julia Rivera, Advanced Graphic Design I, Jennifer Cole Phillips, faculty.

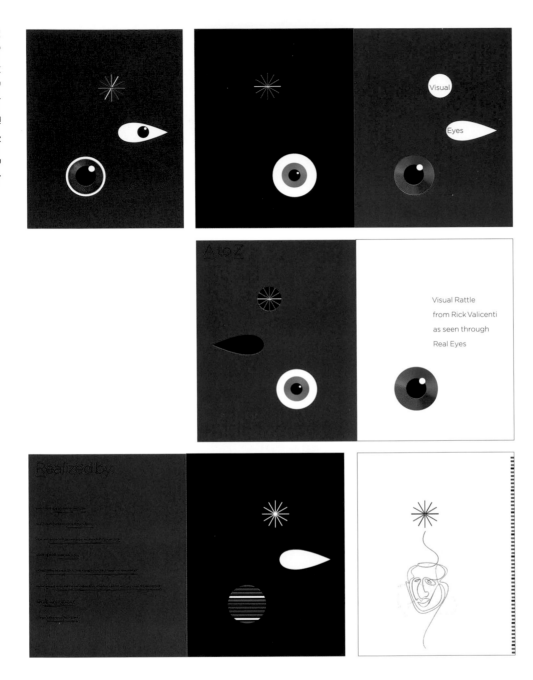

Graceful Entry These pages serve as the cover, lead-in, and close of a lavishly designed and illustrated alphabet book. The simple, well-balanced elements are introduced, then animated with color and context, and finally returned to abstraction, creating a playful and compelling progression that belies the complexity of the book's interior. Rick Valicenti, Thirst.

Beautiful

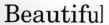

Michael ...s in this book
...m 1976 to 1982
...rietta, Ohio;
...llinois; or
...lle, Virginia.

The pictures
were taken fro...
in either Ma...Northrup
Chicago, I...
Charlottesvi...

l Ecstasy

Spinal Orientation This collection of photographs by Michael Northrup includes many images with a prominent central feature. Designer Paul Sahre responded to this condition by splitting the title and other opening text matter between the front and back of the book, thus creating surprise for and increased interaction with the reader. Paul Sahre, Office of Paul Sahre. Book photographed by Dan Meyers.

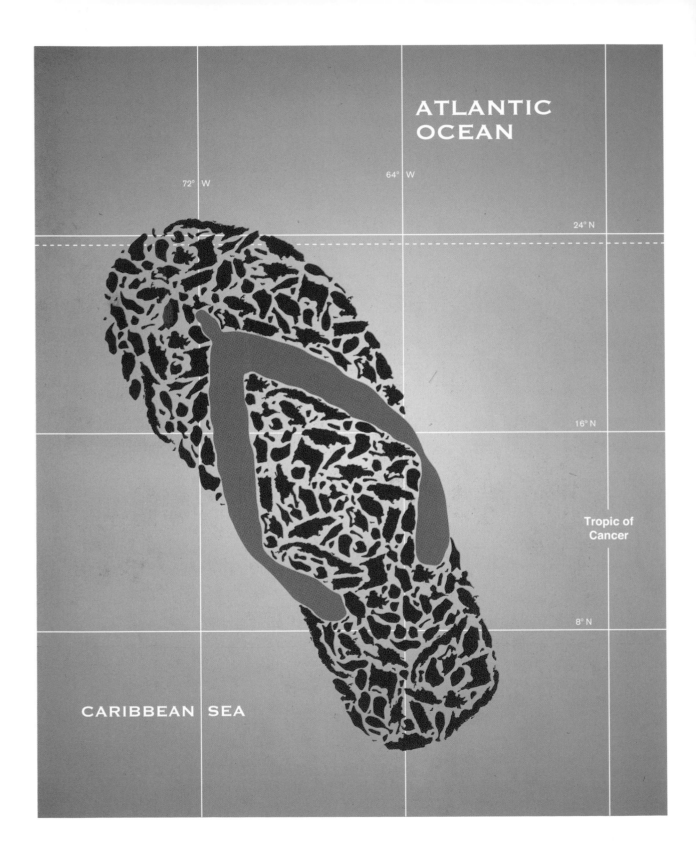

Scale

Miss Darcy was tall, and on **a larger scale** than Elizabeth; and, though little more than sixteen, her figure was formed, and her appearance womanly and graceful. Jane Austen

A printed piece can be as small as a postage stamp or as large as a billboard. A logo must be legible both at a tiny size and from a great distance, while a film might be viewed in a huge stadium or on a handheld device. Some projects are designed to be reproduced at multiple scales, while others are conceived for a single site or medium. No matter what size your work will ultimately be, it must have its own sense of scale.

What do designers mean by scale? Scale can be considered both objectively and subjectively. In objective terms, scale refers to the literal dimensions of a physical object or to the literal correlation between a representation and the real thing it depicts. Printed maps have an exact scale: an increment of measure on the page represents an increment in the physical world. Scale models re-create relationships found in full-scale objects. Thus a model car closely approximates the features of a working vehicle, while a toy car plays with size relationships, inflating some elements while diminishing others.

Subjectively, scale refers to one's impression of an object's size. A book or a room, for example, might have a grand or intimate scale, reflecting how it relates to our own bodies and to our knowledge of other books and other rooms. We say that an image or representation "lacks scale" when it has no cues that connect it to lived experience, giving it a physical identity. A design whose elements all have a similar size often feels dull and static, lacking contrast in scale.

Scale can depend on context. An ordinary piece of paper can contain lettering or images that seem to burst off its edges, conveying a surprising sense of scale. Likewise, a small isolated element can punctuate a large surface, drawing importance from the vast space surrounding it.

Designers are often unpleasantly surprised when they first print out a piece that they have been designing on screen; elements that looked vibrant and dynamic on screen may appear dull and flaccid on the page. For example, 12pt type generally appears legible and appropriately scaled when viewed on a computer monitor, but the same type can feel crude and unwieldy as printed text. Developing sensitivity to scale is an ongoing process for every designer.

Big Picture from Small Parts This design represents Caribbean culture as the colloquy of numerous small islands. The meaning of the image comes directly from the contrast in scale. Robert Lewis, MFA Studio.

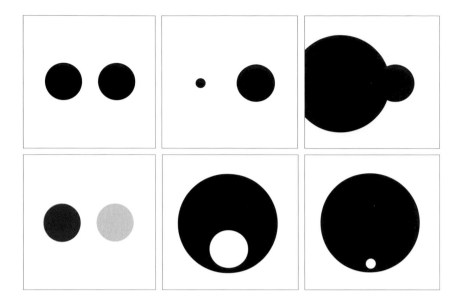

Scale is Relative

A graphic element can appear larger or smaller depending on the size, placement, and color of the elements around it. When elements are all the same size, the design feels flat. Contrast in size can create a sense of tension as well as a feeling of depth and movement. Small shapes tend to recede; large ones move forward.

Cropping to Imply Scale The larger circular form seems especially big because it bleeds off the edges of the page.

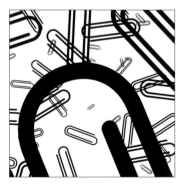

Familiar Objects, Familiar Scale We expect some objects to be a particular scale in relation to each other. Playing with that scale can create spatial illusions and conceptual relationships. Gregory May, MFA Studio.

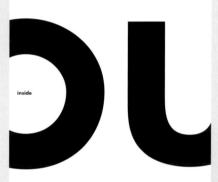

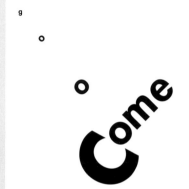

Krista Quick, Nan Yi, Julie Diewald

Jie Lian, Sueyun Choi, Ryan Artell

Jenn Julian, Nan Yi, Sueyun Choi

Scale, Depth, and Motion In the typographic compositions shown here, designers worked with one word or a pair of words and used changes in scale as well as placement on the page to convey the meaning of the word or word pair. Contrasts in scale can imply motion or depth as well as express differences in importance.

Typography I and Graphic Design I.
Ellen Lupton and Zvezdana Rogic, faculty.

Big Type, Small Pages In this book designed by Mieke Gerritzen, the small trim size of the page contrasts with the large-scale type. The surprising size of the text gives the book its loud and zealous voice. The cover is reproduced here at actual size (1:1 scale). Mieke Gerritzen and Geert Lovink, *Mobile Minded*, 2002.

e mobil
le mobi
ile mob
bile mo
obi lem

WHEN WAS THE LAST TIME
I HEARD FROM YOU ANYWAY?

058

MILBI TOY

SEND
SMS

3337772633_
99966668777_
6444663

007

ONLY in JAPAN

WHERE MEN TEND TO VIEW
CELLPHONES AS
TOYS,
WOMAN TREAT THEM LIKE
ACCESSORIES

PERSONALSPACE
JUNKSPACE
VIRTUALSPACE
CELLSPACE
VISUALSPACE
FREESPACE
PUBLICSPACE
NETWO___SPACE
SOC____ACE
COMM____PACE
WOR____ACE
CYBERSPACE
SMARTSPACE
AUGMENTEDSPACE

American reluctance to use mobile phones largely hinges on a highly developed sense of privacy and individuality. Just as people from more social, interconnected cultures see mobiles as a way of extending their networks and adding to their collectivity, many Americans seem to fear that the mobile will undermine their self-reliance and their independence, as well as disturbing their personal space.

THE 1990'S WERE ABOUT THE VIRTUAL:

VIRTUAL REALITY
VIRTUAL WORLDS
CYBERSPACE
AND DOT COMS

The image of an escape into a virtual world which would leave the physical space useless dominated the decade. The new decade brings with it a new emphasis on a physical space augmented with electronic, network and computer technologies: GPG; the omnipresence of video surveillance; "cellspace" applications; objects and buildings sending information to your cellphone or PDA when you are in their vicinity; and gradual dissemination of larger and flatter computer/video displays in public spaces.

SAY GOODBYE,
VIRTUAL SPACE.
PREPARE TO LIVE IN
AUGMENTED SPACE.

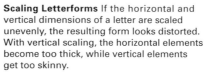

Scale is a Verb

To scale a graphic element is to change its dimensions. Software makes it easy to scale photographs, vector graphics, and letterforms. Changing the scale of an element can transform its impact on the page or screen. Be careful, however: it's easy to distort an element by scaling it disproportionately.

Vector graphics are scalable, meaning that they can be enlarged or reduced without degrading the quality of the image. Bitmap images cannot be enlarged without resulting in a soft or jaggy image.

In two-dimensional animation, enlarging a graphic object over time can create the appearance of a zoom, as if the object were moving closer to the screen.

Scaling Letterforms If the horizontal and vertical dimensions of a letter are scaled unevenly, the resulting form looks distorted. With vertical scaling, the horizontal elements become too thick, while vertical elements get too skinny.

With horizontal scaling, vertical elements become disproportionately heavy, while horizontal elements get thin.

Full-Range Type Family Many typefaces include variations designed with different proportions. The Helvetica Neue type family includes light, medium, bold, and black letters in normal, condensed, and extended widths. The strokes of each letter appear uniform. That effect is destroyed if the letters are unevenly scaled.

| Correct Proportions | Horizontal Scaling | Vertical Scaling |

Scaling Images and Objects Uneven scaling distorts images as well as typefaces. Imagine if you could scale a physical object, stretching or squashing it to make it fit into a particular space. The results are not pretty. Eric Karnes.

Extreme Heights In the poster at right for a lecture at a college, designer Paul Sahre put his typography under severe pressure, yielding virtually illegible results. (He knew he had a captive audience.) Paul Sahre.

PAUL SAHRE: EXERCISES IN FUTILITY, PART IV

APRIL 7, 2000 4PM BUNTING 110 M.I.C.A.

FREE

Texture

If you touch something (it is likely) someone will feel it.
If you feel something (it is likely) **someone will be touched.**
Rick Valicenti

Texture is the tactile grain of surfaces and substances. Textures in our environment help us understand the nature of things: rose bushes have sharp thorns to protect the delicate flowers they surround; smooth, paved roads signal safe passage; thick fog casts a veil on our view.

The textures of design elements similarly correspond to their visual function. An elegant, smoothly patterned surface might adorn the built interior or printed brochure of a day spa; a snaggle of barbed wire could stand as a metaphor for violence or incarceration.

In design, texture is both physical and virtual. Textures include the literal surface employed in the making of a printed piece or physical object as well as the optical appearance of that surface. Paper can be rough or smooth, fabric can be nubby or fine, and packaging material can be glossy or matte. Physical textures affect how a piece feels to the hand, but they also affect how it looks. A smooth or glossy surface, for example, reflects light differently than a soft or pebbly one.

Many of the textures that designers manipulate are not physically experienced by the viewer at all, but exist as optical effect and representation. Texture adds detail to an image, providing an overall surface quality as well as rewarding the eye when viewed up close.

Whether setting type or depicting a tree, the designer uses texture to establish a mood, reinforce a point of view, or convey a sense of physical presence. A body of text set in Garamond italic will have a delicately irregular appearance, while a text set in Univers roman will appear optically smooth with even tonality. Likewise, a smoothly drawn vector illustration will have a different feel from an image taken with a camera or created with code.

As in life, the beauty of texture in design often lies in its poignant juxtaposition or contrast: prickly/soft, sticky/dry, fuzzy/smooth, and so on. By placing one texture in relation to its opposite, or a smart counterpart, the designer can amplify the unique formal properties of each one.

This chapter presents a wide spectrum of textures generated by hand, camera, computer, and code. They are abstract and concrete, and they have been captured, configured, sliced, built, and brushed. They were chosen to remind us that texture has a genuine, visceral, wholly seductive capacity to reel us in and hold us.

High-Tech Finger Paint The letterforms in Rick Valicenti's Touchy Feely alphabet were painted on vertical glass and recorded photographically with a long exposure from a digital, large-format Hasselblad camera. Rick Valicenti, Thirst.

Concrete Texture

The physical quality resulting from repeated slicing, burning, marking, and extracting creates concrete textural surfaces with robust appeal. The studies to the right grew out of a studio exercise where the computer was prohibited in the initial stages of concept and formal development. Turbulence (below), an alphabet by Rick Valicenti, similarly evokes a raw physicality. The alphabet began with vigorous hand-drawn, looping scribbles that were then translated into code.

Surface Manipulation The textural physicality of these type studies artfully reflects the active processes featured in the words. The crisscrossing lines of an artist's cutting board resemble an urban street grid. Jonnie Hallman, Graphic Design I. Bernard Canniffe, faculty.

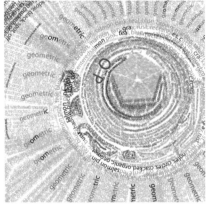

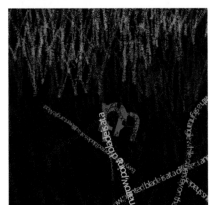

Hayley Griffin

Physical and Virtual Texture
This exercise builds connections between physical and virtual texture (the feel and look of surfaces). Designers used digital cameras to capture compelling textures from the environment. Next, they wrote descriptive paragraphs about each of the textures, focusing on their images' formal characteristics.

Using these descriptive texts as content, the designers re-created the textures typographically in Adobe Illustrator, employing repetition, scale, layers, and color. Typeface selection was open, but scale distortion was not permitted.
Graphic Design I. Mike Weikert, faculty.

Grey Haas

Tim Mason

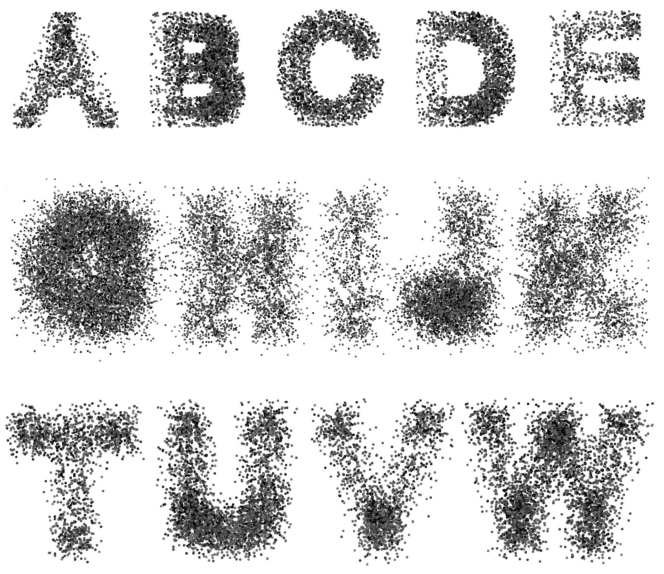

Code-Driven Texture The Swiss typographer Emil Ruder once claimed that vital and individual typographic rhythms are alien to machines. The code-driven letterforms shown here prove otherwise. Generated in the computer language Processing, these forms are effervescent, organic, and, indeed, vital. Yeohyun Ahn, MFA Studio.

Five Squares Ten Inches All typefaces have an innate optical texture that results from the accumulation of attributes such as serifs, slope, stroke width, and proportion. Those attributes interact on the page with the size, tracking, leading, and paragraph style selected by the designer, yielding an overall texture.

In this exercise, designers composed five justified squares of type inside a ten-inch frame. Variation of type style, texture, and value were achieved by combining contrasting characteristics such as old style italic serifs, uniformly weighted sans serifs, geometric slab serifs, and so on. Light to dark value (typographic color) was controlled through the combination of stroke width, letterspacing, and paragraph leading.

Finally, students manipulated the scale and placement of the squares to achieve compositional balance, tension, and depth. Squares were permitted to bleed off the edges, reinforcing the illusion of amplification and recession. Typography I. Jennifer Cole Phillips, faculty.

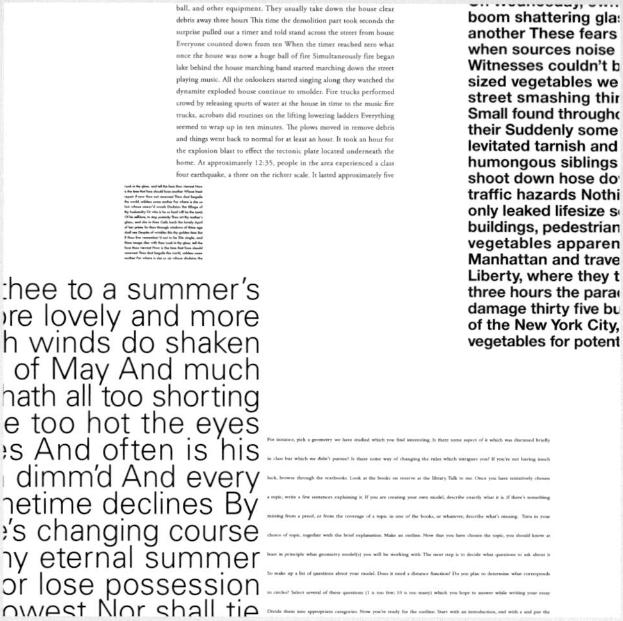

Julie Diewald

Anna Eshelman

iny, that hath to instrument
e never surfeited sea hath
land where man doth not
r unfit to live. I have made
our men hang and drown
ny fellows are ministers of
words are temper'd, may as
bemock'd–at stabs kill the
dowle that's in my plume
erable. If you could hurt
our strengths and will not
ny business to you, that you
Prospero, exposed unto the
s innocent child; for which
rgetting, have incensed the
against your peace. Thee
and do pronounce by me
death can be at once, shall
s, whose wraths to guard
esolate isle, else falls upon
w and a clear life ensuing.

never may believe these antique
fables, nor these fairy toys. Lovers
and madmen have such seething
brains, such shaping fantasies, that
apprehend more than cool reason ever
comprehends. The lunatic, the lover
and the poet are of imagination all
compact. One sees more devils
than vast hell can hold, that is, the
madman. The lover, all as frantic, sees
Helen's beauty in a brow of Egypt: the
poet's eye, in fine frenzy rolling, doth
glance from heaven to earth, from
earth to heaven; and as imagination
bodies forth the forms of things
unknown, the poet's pen turns them
to shapes and gives to airy nothing
a local habitation and a name. Such
tricks hath strong imagination, that if
it would but apprehend some joy, it
comprehends some bringer of that joy.

Anna Eshelman

My mouth tastes like menthol, newly minted coins, and
blood. the flavor of clean. flossed and metallic, french
kissing a robot. You told me something wednesday night
that made me chirp and glow. Do you know you do
that? Your love is one to revel in. You mean so many subtle
things. Like the way wassail burns the back of your throat
but draws you back for more. Like waking up and keeping
your eyes closed and your heartrate low. Like the color of
the sky when it snows. Like that second when the blades
on a ceiling fan finally come to a smooth halt. you embody
everything i have ever known, loved, and stored
in mind If I were a transformer, I'd fold into a cat. Maybe.

My mouth tastes like menthol, newly
minted coins, and blood. the flavor
of clean. flossed and metallic, french
kissing a robot. You told me something
wednesday night that made me chirp
and glow. Do you know you do that?
Your love is one to revel in. You mean
so many subtle things. Like the way
wassail burns the back of your throat.
but draws you back for more. like waking
up and keeping your eyes closed and
your heartrate low. like that second when
the sky when it snows. like that second
when the blades on a ceiling fan
finally come to a smooth halt. you
embody everything I have ever known,
loved, and stored in mind. If I were a
transformer, I'd fold into a cat. Maybe

**My mouth tastes like menthol, newly minted
coins, and blood. the flavor of clean. flossed
and metallic, french kissing a robot. You told
me something wednesday night that made me
chirp and glow. Do you know you do that?
Your love is one to revel in. You mean so
many subtle things. Like the way wassail
burns the back of your throat, but draws you
back for more. like waking up and keeping
your eyes closed and your heartrate low. like
the color of the sky when it snows. like that
second when the blades on a ceiling fan finally
burns the back of your throat, but draws you
back for more. like waking up and keeping
your eyes closed and your heartrate low. like
burns the back of your throat, but draws you
closed and your heartrate low. like come
to a smooth halt. you embody everything**

Ellen Kling

**At the Pentagon, Defense Secretary Donald H
Rumsfeld said that while it was unclear what
role the U.S. military might take in enforcing
new U.N. sanctions, he did not expect the United
States or any other nation to do so unilaterally
At the Pentagon, Defense Secretary Donald H
Rumsfeld said that while it was unclear what
role the U.S. military might take in enforcing
new U.N. sanctions, he did not expect the United
States or any other nation to do so unilaterally
At the Pentagon, Defense Secretary Donald H
Rumsfeld said that while it was unclear what
role the U.S. military might take in enforcing
new U.N. sanctions, he did not expect the United
States or any other nation to do so unilaterally
At the Pentagon, Defense Secretary Donald H
Rumsfeld said that while it was unclear what
role the U.S. military might take in enforcing
new U.N. sanctions, he did not expect the United**

At the Pentagon, Defense Secretary Donald H Rumsfeld
said that while it was unclear what role the U.S. military
might take in enforcing new U.N. sanctions, he did
not expect the United States or any other nation to do so
At the Pentagon, Defense Secretary Donald H Rumsfeld
said that while it was unclear what role the U.S. military
might take in enforcing new U.N. sanctions, he did
not expect the United States or any other nation to do so
At the Pentagon, Defense Secretary Donald H Rumsfeld
said that while it was unclear what role the U.S. military
might take in enforcing new U.N. sanctions, he did
not expect the United States or any other nation to do so
At the Pentagon, Defense Secretary Donald H Rumsfeld
said that while it was unclear what role the U.S. military
might take in enforcing new U.N. sanctions, he did

HyunSoo Lim

On Wednesday, owners and workers downtown
began shattering glass Everyone first feared aald
another These fears were quickly dispelled mad
when sources noise traveled into sight fighters a
Witnesses couldn't believe their eyes Building its
sized vegetables were bouncing down the foxes
street smashing things that got into their water
Small found throughout city had begun vegetable
their Suddenly some unseen force dervish fusion
levitated tarnish and into the streets water cared
humongous siblings Fire trucks and cops sandy
shoot down hose down, and rope down every an
traffic hazards Nothing worked. vegetables alter
only leaked lifesize seeds tons of juice onto most
buildings, pedestrians streets. The parade of lost
vegetables apparently was first spotted upper
Manhattan and traveled all the way to the Statue
Liberty, where they then moved out to sea. Mast
three hours the parade had managed structurally
damage thirty five buildings, scare the population
of the New York City, and leave them without add
vegetables for potentially a week :) scary thought

day Thou art more lovely and m
temperate Rough winds do sha
the darling buds of May And sc
summer's lease hath all too shor
a date Sometime too hot the e
of heaven shines And often is
gold complexion dimm'd And ev
fair from fair sometime declines
chance or nature's changing cou
untrimm'd But thy eternal summ
shall not fade Nor lose possess
of that fair thou owest Nor shal
Death brag thou wander'st in th
shade When in eternal lines to t
thou growest So long as men ca
breathe or eyes can see So long
lives this and this gives life to th

ss, and tell the face thou viewest Now
face should form another Whose fresh
thou not renewest Thou dost beguile
less some mother For where is she so
ear'd womb Disdains the tillage of
Or who is he so fond will be the tomb
, to stop posterity Thou art thy mother's
e in thee Calls back the lovely April
o thou through windows of thine age
ite of wrinkles this thy golden time But
member'd not to be Die single, and
es with thee Look in thy glass, tell the

Julie Diewald

Wenji Lu

Typographic Portraits This exploration of typographic texture begins with a basic black-and-white photograph. Designers translate the tonal and textural qualities using only typographic variables, such as weight, style, size, alignment, and spacing, to approximate their own likeness. Solutions range from tightly articulated to loosely expressive and are built from words mined from the students' biographies. Graduate Typography. Jennifer Cole Phillips, faculty.

Yushi Luo

Katrina Keane

Lolo Zhang

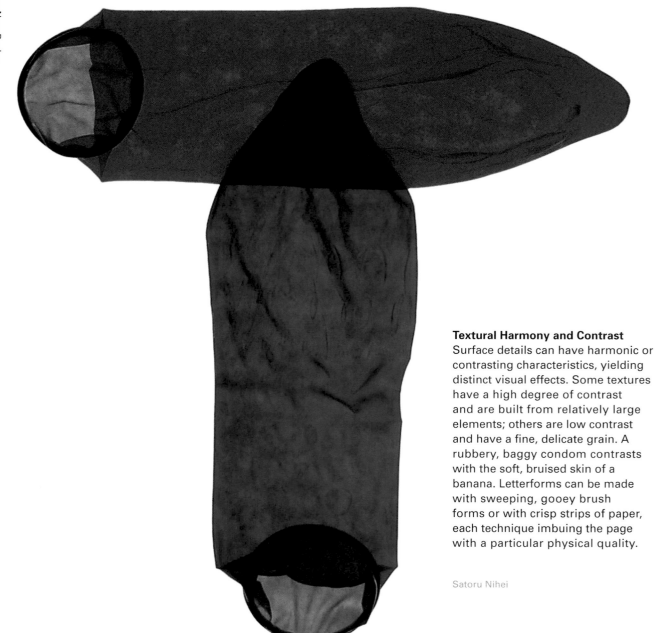

Textural Harmony and Contrast
Surface details can have harmonic or contrasting characteristics, yielding distinct visual effects. Some textures have a high degree of contrast and are built from relatively large elements; others are low contrast and have a fine, delicate grain. A rubbery, baggy condom contrasts with the soft, bruised skin of a banana. Letterforms can be made with sweeping, gooey brush forms or with crisp strips of paper, each technique imbuing the page with a particular physical quality.

Satoru Nihei

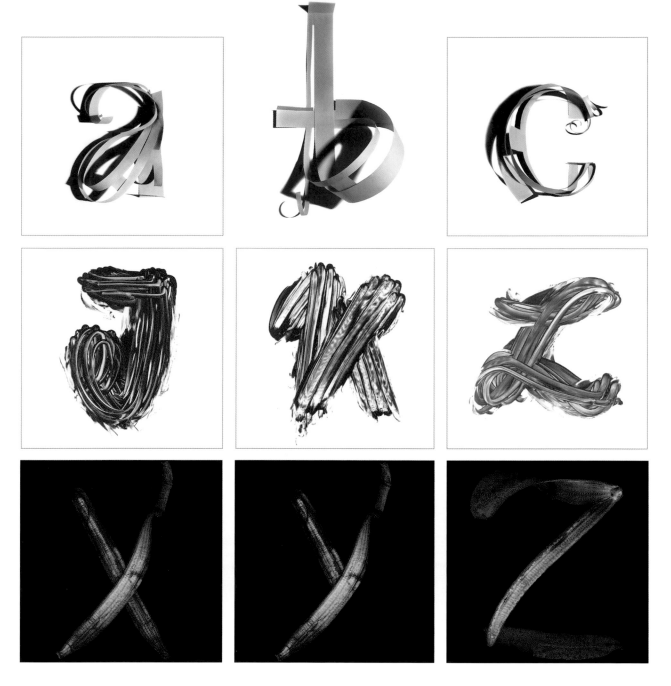

Alphabetic Texture These alphabets are from a diverse collection created for Rick Valicenti's Playground experiment, where letters are constructed from physical objects and processes. Designers top to bottom: Michelle Bowers, Rick Valicenti, Jenn Stucker.

Color

All colors are the friends of their neighbors and the **lovers of their opposites**. Marc Chagall

Color can convey a mood, describe reality, or codify information. Words like "gloomy," "drab," and "glittering" each bring to mind a general climate of colors, a palette of relationships. Designers use color to make some things stand out (warning signs) and to make other things disappear (camouflage). Color serves to differentiate and connect, to highlight and to hide.

Graphic design was once seen as a fundamentally black-and-white enterprise. This is no longer the case. Color has become integral to the design process. Color printing, once a luxury, has become routine. An infinite range of hues and intensities bring modern media to life, energizing the page, the screen, and the built environment with sensuality and significance. Graphics and color have converged.

According to the classical tradition, the essence of design lies in linear structures and tonal relationships (drawing and shading), not in fleeting optical effects (hue, intensity, luminosity). Design used to be understood as an abstract armature that underlies appearances. Color, in contrast, was seen as subjective and unstable.

And, indeed, it is. Color exists, literally, in the eye of the beholder. We cannot perceive color until light bounces off an object or is emitted from a source and enters the eye.

Our perception of color depends not solely on the pigmentation of physical surfaces, but also on the brightness and character of ambient light. We also perceive a given color in relation to the other colors around it. For example, a light tone looks lighter against a dark ground than against a pale one.

Likewise, color changes meaning from culture to culture. Colors carry different connotations in different societies. White signals virginity and purity in the West, but it is the color of death in Eastern cultures. Red, worn by brides in Japan, is considered racy and erotic in Europe and the United States. Colors go in and out of fashion, and an entire industry has emerged to guide and predict its course.

To say, however, that color is a shifting phenomenon—both physically and culturally—is not to say that it can't be described or understood. A precise vocabulary has been established over time that makes it possible for designers, software systems, printers, and manufacturers to communicate to one another with some degree of clarity. This chapter outlines the basic terms of color theory and shows ways to build purposeful relationships among colors.

Opposites Attract Strong color contrasts add visual energy to this dense physical montage made from flowers. Blue and purple stand out against pink, orange, and red. Nancy Froehlich and Zvezdana Rogic.

Basic Color Theory

In 1665 Sir Isaac Newton discovered that a prism separates light into the spectrum of colors: red, orange, yellow, green, blue, indigo, and violet. He organized the colors around a wheel very much like the one artists use today to describe the relationships among colors.[1]

Why is the color wheel a useful design tool? Colors that sit near each other on the spectrum or close together on the color wheel are analogous. Using them together provides minimal color contrast and an innate harmony, because each color has some element in common with others in the sequence. Analogous colors also have a related color temperature. Two colors sitting opposite each other on the wheel are complements. Each color contains no element of the other, and they have opposing temperatures (warm versus cool). Deciding to use analogous or contrasting colors affects the visual energy and mood of any composition.

Secondaries and Complements This series of posters is produced with complements (orange + blue) and two secondary colors (orange + purple). Mixes and gradients provide the steps in between. Richard Blake, MFA Studio.

1. On basic color theory and practice, see Tom Fraser and Adam Banks, *Designer's Color Manual* (San Francisco: Chronicle Books, 2004).

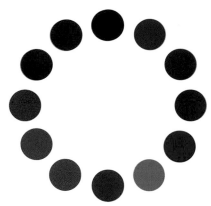

The Color Wheel
This basic map shows relationships among colors. Children learn to mix colors according to this model, and artists use it for working with pigments (oil paint, watercolor, gouache, and so on).

Primary Colors
Red, yellow, and blue are pure; they can't be mixed from other colors. All of the other colors on the wheel are created by mixing primary colors.

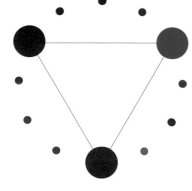

Secondary Colors
Orange, purple, and green each consist of two primaries mixed together.

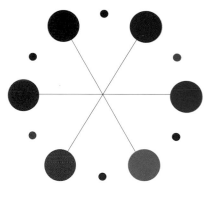

Tertiary Colors
Colors such as red orange and yellow green are mixed from one primary and one secondary color.

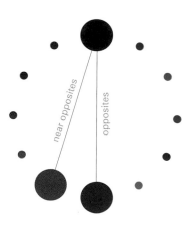

Complements
Red/green, blue/orange, and yellow/purple sit opposite each other on the color wheel. For more subtle combinations, choose near opposites, such as red plus a tertiary green, or a tertiary blue and a tertiary orange.

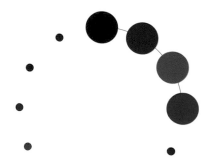

Analogous Colors
Color schemes built from hues that sit near to each other on the color wheel (analogous colors) have minimal chromatic differences.

Hue is the place of
the color within the
spectrum. A red hue
can look brown at
a low saturation, or
pink at a pale value.

Intensity is the brightness or dullness
of a color. A color is made duller by
adding black or white, as well as by
neutralizing it toward gray (lowering
its saturation).

Value is the light or dark character of the
color, also called its luminance, brightness,
lightness, or tone. Value is independent of
the hue or intensity of the color. When you
convert a color image to black and white,
you eliminate its hue but preserve its tonal
relationships.

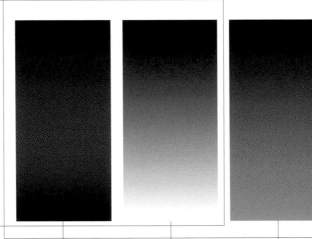

Aspects of Color

Every color can be described in
relation to a range of attributes.
Understanding these characteristics
can help you make color choices
and build color combinations. Using
colors with contrasting values tends
to bring forms into sharp focus,
while combining colors that are
close in value softens the distinction
between elements.

Shade is a variation
of a hue produced by
the addition of black.

Tint is a variation of
a hue produced by
the addition of white.

Saturation (also
called chroma) is the
relative purity of the
color as it neutralizes
to gray.

These colors are
close in value
and intensity, and
just slightly
different in hue.

These colors are
close in hue and
value but different
in intensity.

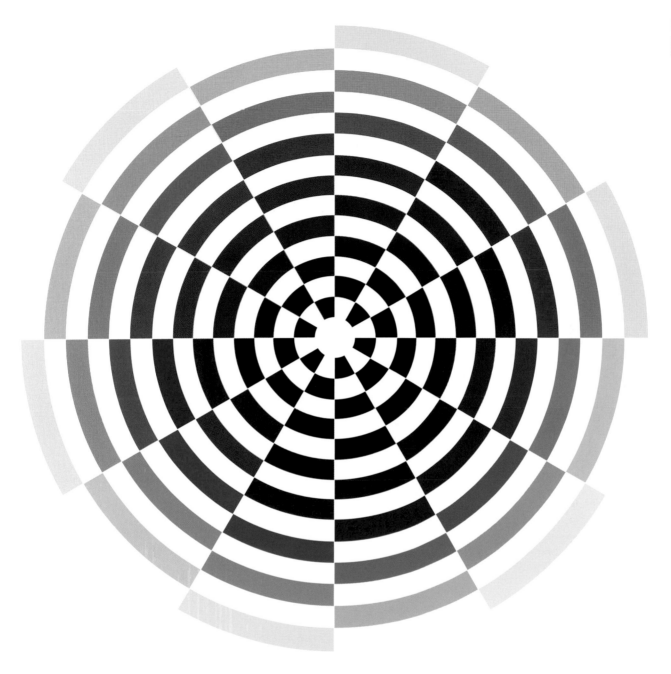

Graduated Color Wheel Each hue on the color wheel is shown here in a progressive series of values (shades and tints). Note that the point of greatest saturation is not the same for each hue. Yellow is of greatest intensity toward the lighter end of the value scale, while blue is more intense in the darker zone.

Use the graduated color wheel to look for combinations of colors that are similar in value or saturation, or use it to build contrasting relationships. Robert Lewis, MFA Studio.

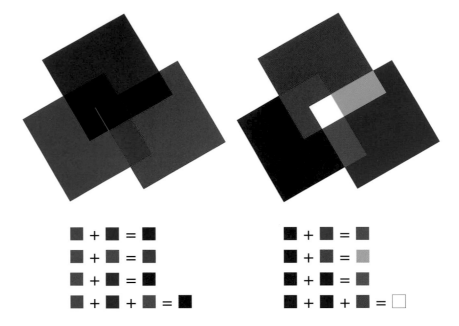

Color Models

Surfaces absorb certain light waves and reflect back others onto the color receptors (cones) in our eyes. The light reflected back is the light we see. The true primaries of visible light are red, green, and blue. The light system is called "additive" because the three primaries together create all the hues in the spectrum.

In theory, combining red and green paint should produce yellow. In practice, however, these pigments combine into a blackish brown. This is because pigments absorb more light than they reflect, making any mix of pigments darker than its source colors. As more colors are mixed, less light is reflected. Thus pigment-based color systems are called "subtractive."

Offset and desktop printing methods use CMYK, a subtractive system. Nonstandard colors are used because the light reflected off cyan and magenta pigments mixes more purely into new hues than the light reflected off of blue and red pigments.

CYMK is used in the printing process. While painters use the basic color wheel as a guide for mixing paint, printing ink uses a different set of colors: cyan, magenta, yellow, and black, which are ideal for reproducing the range of colors found in color photographs. C, M, Y, and K are known as the "process colors," and full-color printing is called "four-color process." Ink-jet and color laser printers use CMYK, as does the commercial offset printing equipment used to print books such as this one.

In principle, C, M, and Y should produce black, but the resulting mix is not rich enough to reproduce color images with a full tonal range. Thus black is needed to complete the four-color process.

RGB is the additive system used for designing on screen. Different percentages of red, green, and blue light combine to generate the colors of the spectrum. White occurs when all three colors are at full strength. Black occurs when zero light (and thus zero color) is emitted.

Any given color can be described with both CMYK and RGB values, as well as with other color models. Each model (called a "color space") uses numbers to convey color information uniformly around the globe and across media. Different monitors, printing conditions, and paper stocks all affect the appearance of the final color, as does the light in the environment where the color is viewed. Colors look different under fluorescent, incandescent, and natural light. Colors rarely translate perfectly from one space to another.

Transparent Ink Printer's inks are transparent, so color mixing occurs as colors show through each other. Color mixing is also performed optically when the image is broken down into tiny dots of varying size. The resulting colors are mixed by the eye.

Transparent Light The medium of light is also transparent. The colors of an emitted image are generated when different colors of light mix directly, as well as when tiny adjacent pixels combine optically.

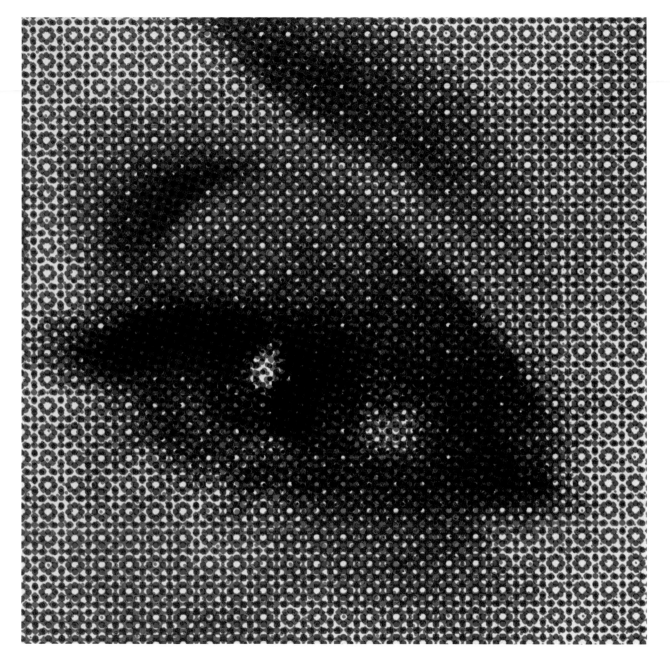

Optical Color Mixing This detail from a printed paper billboard shows the principle of four-color process printing (CMYK). Viewed from a distance, the flecks of color mix together optically. Seen up close, the pattern of dots is strongly evident.

Whatever color model your software is using, if you are viewing it on screen, it is RGB. If you are viewing it in print, it is CMYK.

One Color, Different Effects The neutral tone passing through these three squares of color is the same in each instance. It takes on a slightly different hue or value depending on its context.

Bezold Effect Johann Friedrich Wilhelm von Bezold was a German physicist working in the nineteenth century. Fascinated with light and color, he also was an amateur rug maker. He noticed that by changing a color that interwove with other colors in a rug, he could create entirely different results. Adding a darker color to the carpet would create an overall darker effect, while adding a lighter one yielded a lighter carpet. This effect is known as optical mixing.

Interaction of Color

Josef Albers, a painter and designer who worked at the Bauhaus before emigrating to the United States, studied color in a rigorous manner that influenced generations of art educators.[2] Giving his students preprinted sheets of colored paper with which to work, he led them to analyze and experience how the perception of color changes in relation to how any given color is juxtaposed with others.

Colors are mixed in the eye as well as directly on the painter's palette or the printing press. This fact affects how designers create patterns and textures, and it is exploited in digital and mechanical printing methods, which use small flecks of pure hue to build up countless color variations.

Designers juxtapose colors to create specific climates and qualities, using one color to diminish or intensify another. Understanding how colors interact helps designers control the power of color and systematically test variations of an idea.

Vibration and Value When two colors are very close in value, a glowing effect occurs; on the left, the green appears luminous and unstable. With a strong value difference, as seen on the right, the green appears darker.

2. See Josef Albers, *Interaction of Color* (1963; repr., New Haven: Yale University Press, 2006).

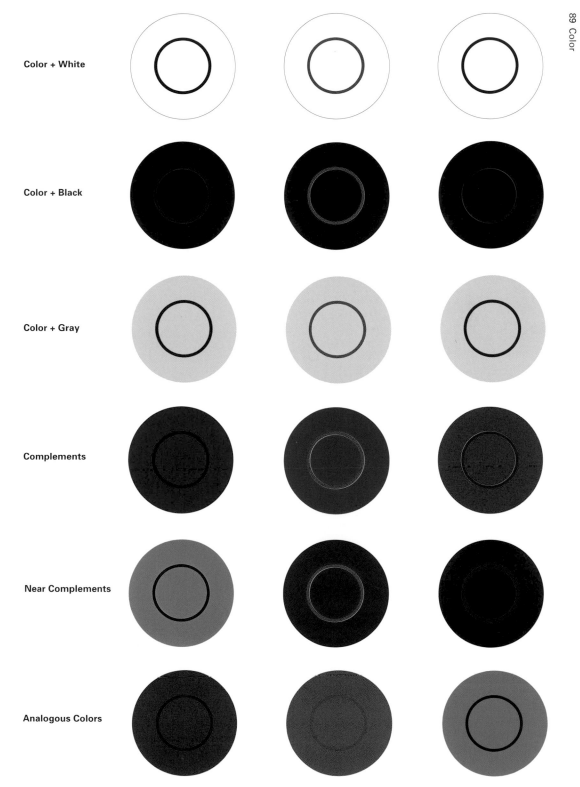

Color + White

Color + Black

Color + Gray

Complements

Near Complements

Analogous Colors

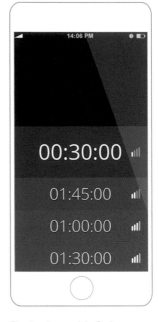
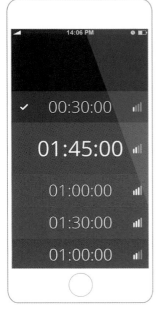
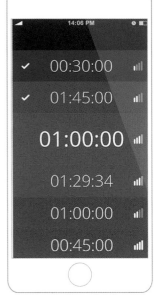

Designing with Color

Whereas a painter often produces dozens of colors in a spontaneous manner, designers work with color more systematically. Rather than mix colors on the fly, they often select them from libraries of swatches and define colors as global values across a project. Colors take on specific functions within a design project. Many brand campaigns, websites, posters, signage, and other graphics employ a limited number of colors that cover a range of values and color temperatures. A palette might consist of black, white, and one or two accent colors. By occupying a middle ground between black and white, an accent color can allow type to appear in both black and white, adding to a piece's typographic range. Including both warm and cool hues in a color palette creates a sense of visual completeness, like a salad with a full range of flavors and textures. Even though digital media enable designers to use numerous colors at no additional cost, creating color systems still supports strong communication.

Blue + Yellow = Green This design for an app that tracks the duration and intensity of cardio workouts uses a stepped range of colors to communicate information in a direct and understandable way. Alex Jacque, MFA Studio.

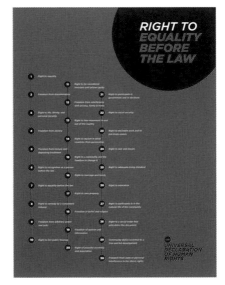

Black + One The yellow is deep enough to allow the white type to read against it.

Black + Two The warm salmon red and cool greenish blue bring a satisfying sense of completeness to the palette. Michael Shillingburg, Typography II. Ellen Lupton, faculty.

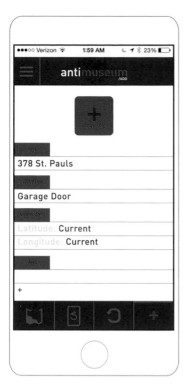
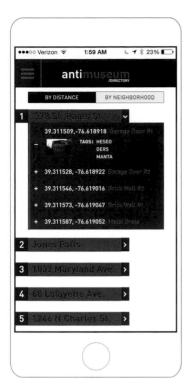

Black Is a Color This interface uses a minimal color range to convey simple actions. Used richly and forcefully, the black and gray tones become full-fledged actors within the color palette. Michael Bonfiglio, MFA Studio.

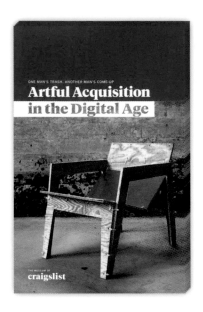

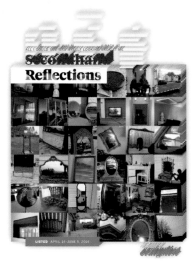

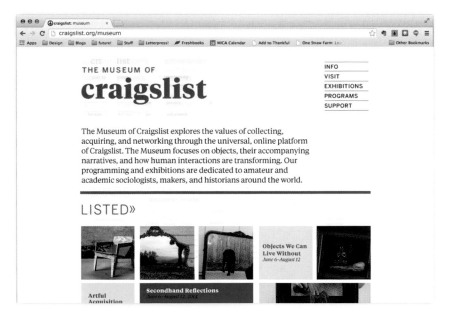

Monochrome A single shade of blue expresses a no-nonsense attitude in this branding project. Lighter shades of blue and mixtures of blue and black express a broad range of tonality within a limited spectrum. Amanda Buck, MFA Studio.

Hard Light This museum identity contrasts
an intense, cold blue with pure red to
reference the RGB color space. Katrina Keane,
MFA Studio.

Hot and Cold Simple primary colors serve as
a background for black-and-white typography.
Shiva Nallaperumal, MFA Studio.

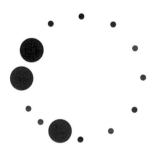

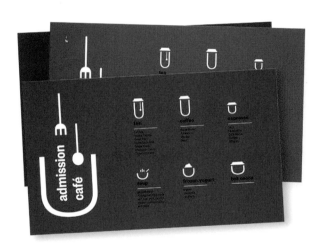

Analogous Naturals The three colors that make up the palette of this museum branding project come from positions located near each other on the color wheel. The gently muted, desaturated hues convey an organic quality. Iris Sprague, MFA Studio.

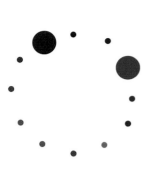

Near Complements The rosy orange and deep violet featured in this brand identity sit near each other on the color wheel, creating harmony within a range of warm and cool. Louis Luo, MFA Studio.

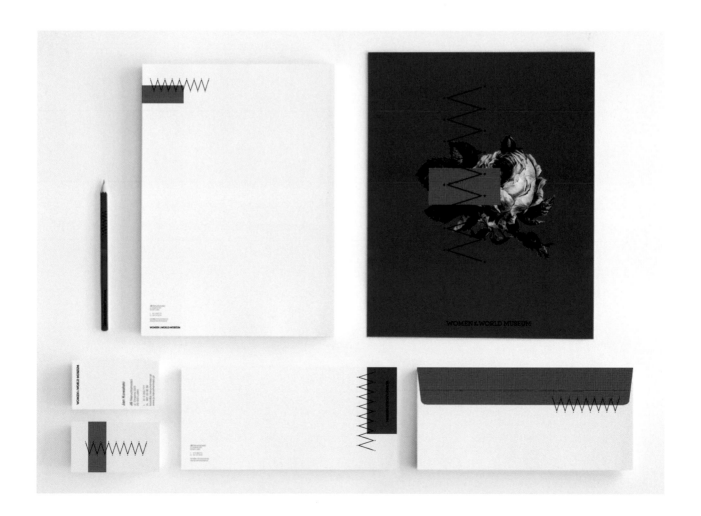

Joanna Marshall

Katie Evans

Ellen Kling

Elizabeth Tipson

Neutral earth tones combine to make a quiet overall pattern, while a palette with strong contrasts of value and hue yields a more linear effect.

By changing the colors of background and foreground elements, completely new forms appear and disappear.

Colors close in value but different in hue create a vibrant yet soft effect. The pattern becomes even softer when analogous colors are used.

Selective Emphasis These studies use typographic patterns to explore how color alters not just the mood of a pattern, but the way its shapes and figures are perceived. Color affects both the parts and the whole. Each study begins with a black and white pattern built from a single font and letterform.

Experiments with hue, value, and saturation, as well as with analogous, complementary, and near complementary color juxtapositions, affect the way the patterns feel and behave. Through selective emphasis, some elements pull forward and others recede. Typography I. Jennifer Cole Phillips, faculty.

Passion, Palettes, and Products What began as a love for Portuguese tile patterns on a trip to Lisbon evolved into an intensive investigation into pattern, form, and color, manifesting itself in an MFA thesis project and now an online business.

Textile designers often create numerous colorways for a single pattern, allowing the same printing plates or weaving templates to generate diverse patterns. Different color palettes make different elements of the pattern come forward or recede. Jessica Pilar, MFA Studio.

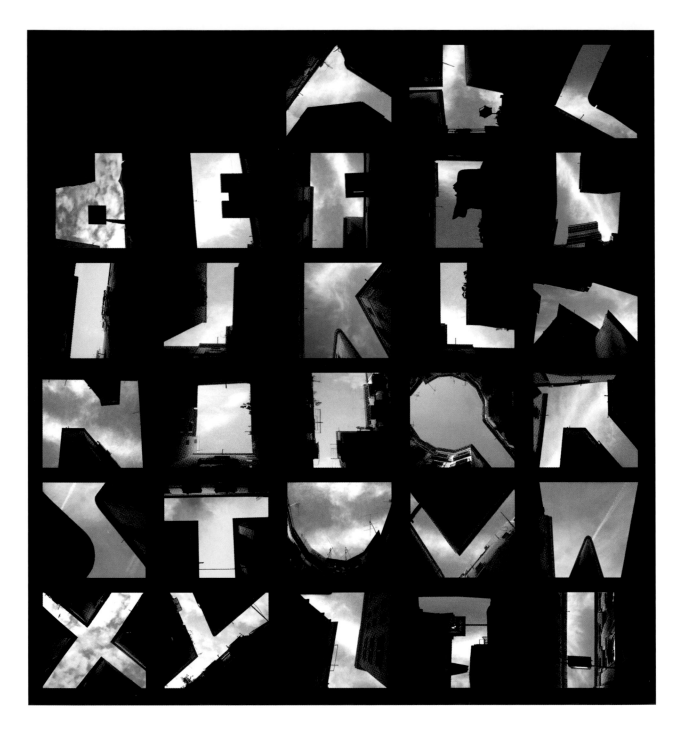

Gestalt Principles

The form of an object is not more important than the form of the space surrounding it. **All things exist in interaction with other things.** In music, are the separations between notes less important than the notes themselves? Malcolm Grear

Perception is an active process. Human cognition simplifies an enormous range of stimuli into understandable units. The myriad colors, shapes, textures, sounds, and movements that confront us from moment to moment would be overwhelming and incomprehensible if the brain didn't structure the so-called sense data into coherent objects and patterns. The brain actively breaks down and combines sensory input. It merges what we see with what we know to build a coherent understanding of the world. Building on memory and experience, the brain fills in gaps and filters out extraneous data.

By exploiting the brain's capacity to find and create order, designers construct simple, direct logos, layouts, and interfaces. In addition to seeking out clear, direct communication solutions, they can also use the processes of perception to invent surprising forms that challenge viewers to fill in the gaps.

Visual perception is shaped by figure/ground relationships.

We separate figures (forms) from the space, color, or patterns that surround them (ground, or background). We see letters against a page, a building in relation to its site, and a sculpture against the void that penetrates and surrounds it. A black shape on a black field is not visible; without separation and contrast, form disappears.

People are accustomed to seeing the background as passive and unimportant in relation to a dominant subject. Yet visual artists become attuned to the spaces around and between elements, discovering their power to become active forms in their own right.

Graphic designers often seek a balance between figure and ground, using this relationship to bring energy and order to form and space. They build contrasts between form and counterform in order to construct icons, illustrations, logos, compositions, and patterns that stimulate the eye and mind. Creating ambiguity between figure and ground can add visual energy and surprise to an image or mark.

Figure/ground, also known as positive and negative space, is at work in all facets of graphic design. When creating logotypes and symbols, designers often distill complex meaning into simplified but significant form; the resulting marks often thrive on the interplay between figure and ground, solid and void. In posters, layouts, and screen designs, what is left out frames and balances explicit forms.

The ability to create and evaluate effective figure/ground tension is an essential skill for graphic designers. Train your eye to carve out white space as you compose with forms. Learn to massage the positive and negative areas as you adjust the scale of images and typography. Look at the shapes each element makes, and see if the edges frame a void that is equally appealing.

Recognizing the potency of the ground, designers strive to reveal its constructive necessity. Working with grouping, patterns, and figure/ground relationships gives designers the power to create—and destabilize—form.

Figure Sky These photographs use urban buildings to frame letterforms. The empty sky becomes the dominant figure, and the buildings become the background that makes them visible. Lisa Rienermann, University of Essen, Germany.

Bubble Dot Typeface
The letters of
the alphabet are so
ingrained in our
memory that they are
still recognizable
when fragmented
or distorted. Typeface
by Cornel Windlin.

Sense Data + Experience

In the act of perception, the brain puts together past experience and immediate sensory input in order to successfully navigate the environment. We know a chair has four legs, even when some of them are hiding. When we see the top part of a face, we reasonably expect a mouth and chin to follow. Designers crop, overlap, and fragment images to create dynamic forms that exploit the brain's powerful ability to fill in missing information.

Typography is an especially powerful system of sensory objects. Because reading is such a deeply ingrained habit, we immediately recognize the shapes of letterforms. It is difficult not to read a word sitting in front of us. Yet letterforms are also abstract symbols built from lines and curves. They make no sense outside the regime of literacy. By blocking, cutting, or distorting letterforms, designers exploit the tension between meaning and abstraction, familiarity and strangeness.

Perception isn't just visual.[1] As we walk through a city street or shady forest, layers of sound surround us. We navigate this complex sensory environment by intuitively associating sounds with objects, from the drumbeat of footsteps to the song of a bird and the shriek of an ambulance.

How Many Cars? We perceive two cars, a red car and a blue car, even though our sensory information about the red car is incomplete.

How Many Legs? Based on our knowledge of chairs as well as the sense data provided by the picture, we intuit that each chair has four legs.

The Power of the Gaze
The human brain is keenly attuned to facial features, especially eyes. Designers often focus our attention on the eyes. Blocking the eyes can create emotional tension.

1. For an outstanding introduction to the science of perception, see Michael Haverkamp, *Synesthetic Design: Handbook for a Multisensory Approach* (Basel: Birkhäuser, 2013).

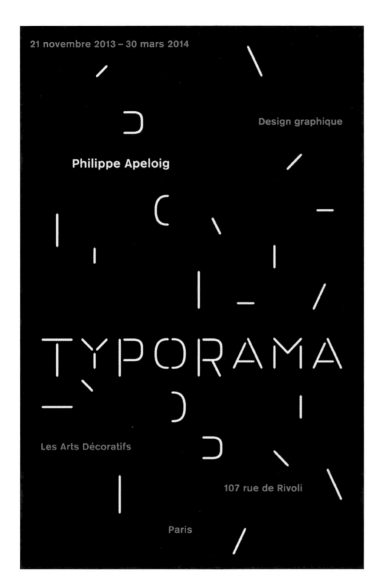

Fill in the Blanks Our brain connects the parts back into wholes in this logotype for an exhibition. Philippe Apeloig.

Denying Eye Contact The blocked eyes produce a sense of psychological erasure. Paula Scher, Pentagram.

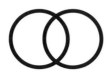

Simplicity We see two circles rather than three odd shapes.

Similarity We see two groups based on the size of the elements.

Proximity We see two groups based on the closeness of the elements.

Closure We close the gap in the shape.

Continuity We see two long lines crossing rather than four short lines converging.

Symmetry We tend to close symmetrical forms to make a single object.

Grouping

In human perception, grouping serves to both combine and separate. As a process of combining, grouping transforms multiple elements into larger entities based on size, shape, color, proximity, and other factors. For example, we might group three blue circles and three yellow circles into two clusters. Interface designers use the principle of grouping to color-code buttons with related functions (similarity) as well as to position related buttons close together (proximity).

As a process of separating, grouping serves to break down large, complex objects into smaller, simpler ones. When we simplify criss-crossing marks into a few overlapping lines or shapes, the mind turns complex sensory input into more manageable objects.

Project: Six Modes of Grouping

Psychologists have identified various principles of grouping; six common ones are diagrammed above. Designers often manipulate one or more principles of grouping in order to create images or compositions that are clear and focused or unsettled and surprising. Interesting effects emerge when we use our powers of perception to reassemble lines, shapes, or images that have been pulled apart or interrupted. Grouping prompts the observer to build parts into wholes.

Designers were challenged to create a series of diagrams that use a common language of line, shape, scale, and/or color to demonstrate six principles of grouping. As a starting point, designers researched the range of diagrams typically used by psychologists to demonstrate these principles, such as those shown above. Nick Fogarty, Laura Brewer-Yarnal, Angel Kim, Trace Byrd, Typography II. Ellen Lupton, faculty.

Grouped for Function This digital control panel groups related actions together.

Simplicity

Similarity

Proximity

Closure

Continuity

Symmetry

   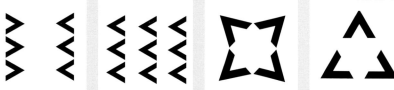

Simplicity   **Similarity**   **Proximity**   **Closure**   **Continuity**   **Symmetry**

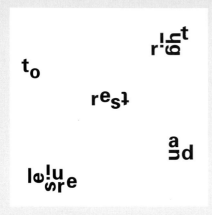

Proximity The disordered letters cluster together to form words. Devon Burgoyne.

Continuity The converging words read as two lines crossing. Laura Brewer-Yarnall.

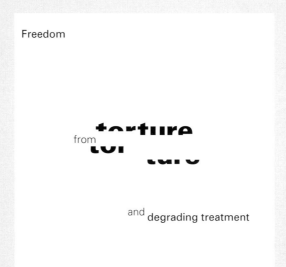

Closure Our powers of perception close the gaps in the letterforms. Angel Kim.

Project: Grouping + Typography
At its most basic level, all typography employs principles of grouping. Letters cluster into words (*proximity*). Shifts in weight, style, or size signal differences and hierarchies (*similarity*). When we create "lines" of text out of letters and words, we exploit the power of *continuity*, which sustains the illusion of a single gesture or path.

This project encourages designers to experiment with the basic principles of typography.

Each student creates multiple interpretations of a given text by using spacing, composition, and alignment. Designers explore the impact of principles such as proximity, similarity, continuity, and closure to create new patterns of meaning that exploit the mind's ability to reconnect fragments and build wholes out of parts. The text in this project comes from the Bill of Universal Human Rights. Typography II. Ellen Lupton, faculty.

Proximity The letters in this neo-Dada poster have been scrambled and mismatched, yet they still read as words because they cluster into groups. Designers United.

Broken Curves The lines break into panels of color wherever they cross over other lines, yet our powers of perception make them hold together. Felix Pfäffli, Feixen.

Similarity The words have been split apart across the surface of the poster, but color helps reunite the parts. Felix Wetzel.

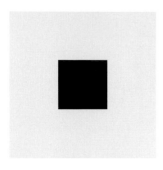

Stable

Reversible

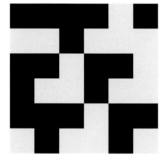

Ambiguous

Figure/Ground

A stable figure/ground relationship exists when a form or figure stands clearly apart from its background. Most photography functions according to this principle, where an obvious subject is featured within a setting.

Reversible figure/ground occurs when positive and negative elements attract our attention equally and alternately. In stripes of equal width, each set of lines can come forward or recede as our eye perceives it first as dominant and then as subordinate. Reversible figure/ground motifs appear in ceramics, weaving, and crafts produced in cultures across history and around the globe.

Images and compositions featuring ambiguous figure/ground challenge the viewer to find a stable focal point. Figure flows into ground, carrying the viewer's eye in and around the surface with no discernible assignment of dominance. Cubist paintings mobilize this ambiguity.

Interwoven Space

Designers, illustrators, and photographers often play with figure/ground relationships to add interest and intrigue to their work. Unlike conventional depictions where subjects are centered and framed against a background, active figure/ground conditions churn and interweave form and space, creating tension and ambiguity.

Optical Interplay This mark for Vanderbilt University employs a strong contrast between rigid form and organic counterform. The elegant oak leaf alternately sinks back, allowing the letterform to read, and comes forward, connoting growth, strength, and beauty. Malcolm Grear, Malcolm Grear Designers.

The Guggenheim Museum

Artful Reduction A minimal stack of carefully shaped forms, in concert with exacting intervals of spaces, instantly evokes this architectural landmark. Malcolm Grear, Malcolm Grear Designers.

Concept Sketching

Fast, informal visualizations allow designers to explore different figure/ground relationships in a low-risk environment that fosters invention and discovery. While verbalizing ideas helps designers build a bank of potential concepts, sketching pushes these ideas closer to reality. Multiple sketches yield a more valuable process than single sketches, as drawings begin to speak to one another, opening the mind and eye to new connections.

Search and Find The designer explored multiple iterations of core symbols in order to create emotionally charged icons that compress multiple ideas into a single image. Chen Yu, The Illustrated Poster.

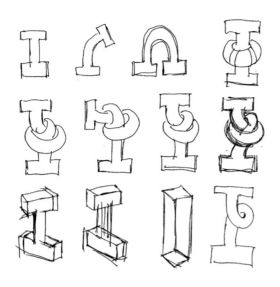

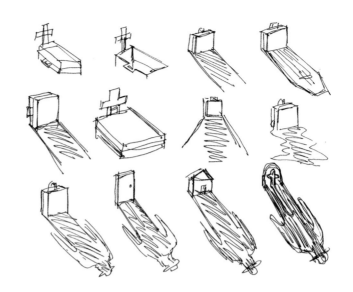

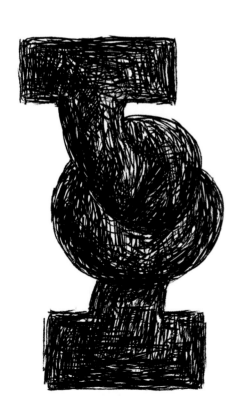

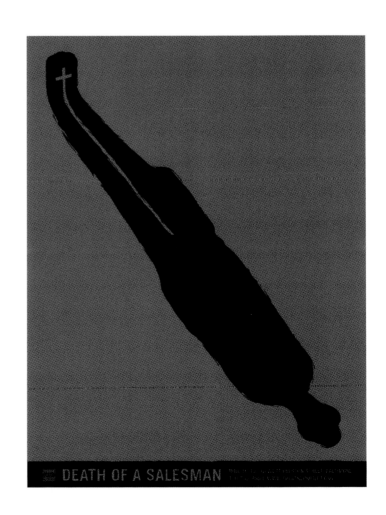

DEATH OF A SALESMAN

Letterform Abstraction In this introduction to letterform anatomy, students examined the forms and counterforms of the alphabet in many font variations, eventually isolating just enough of each letter to hint at its identity. Each student sought to strike a balance between positive and negative space. Typography I. Jennifer Cole Phillips, faculty.

Is Negative Space a Privilege of the Rich? This poster (opposite page) challenges designers' attraction to "white space" by analyzing (and materializing) the distribution of unprinted areas in magazines designed to appeal to readers with different levels of wealth. Sally Maier, MFA Studio.

White Space is a Luxury Good

AVG. HOUSEHOLD INCOME OF READERSHIP

$166,391 / €123.389
New York Times
Style Magazine

$93,960 / €69.677
RealSimple

$57,716 / €42.800
Ladies Home Journal

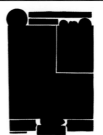

$39,626 / €29.385
OK! magazine

Retouched Figure becomes ground and interface becomes image in this poster about digital manipulation. Shiva Nallaperumal, MFA Studio. Winner, 4th Biennial Graphic Design Festival, Breda, Netherlands.

Trafficked Luggage tags represent proof of ownership when baggage is moved from one destination to another via modern transportation networks. In this poster about the scourge of human trafficking, a female figure has been cut from a luggage tag, taking shape as negative space. This vulnerable, voided body has been stripped of identity. The bar code is scannable, linking readers to critical information about the magnitude and economics of human trafficking. The poster was exhibited in the Netherlands, a country where prostitution is legal and trafficking is endemic. *Katrina Kean, MFA Studio. Winner, 4th Biennial Graphic Design Festival, Breda, Netherlands.*

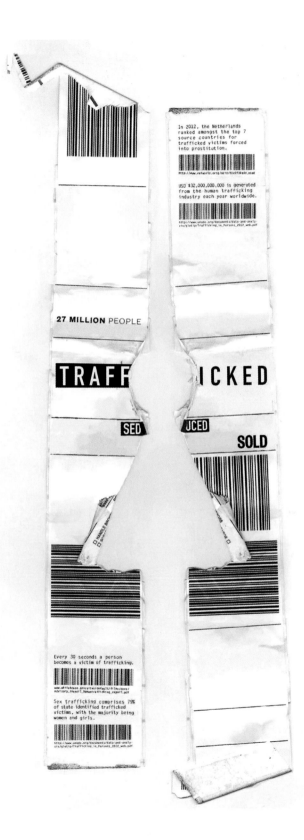

No Entry These crudely punched letters are readable against the sky and sea, whose contrasting value lights up the message. Jayme Odgers.

Counter Hand The simple device of cut white paper held against a contrasting ground defines the alphabet with quirky style and spatial depth. FWIS Design.

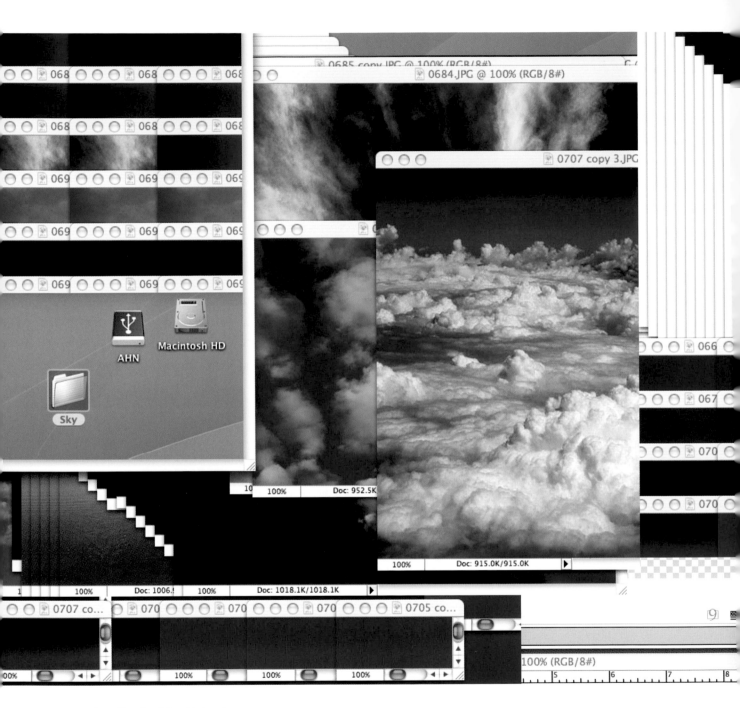

Interface Overload Graphic interfaces are a constant presence throughout the design process. Here, the interface itself—and its excessive accumulation of windows—becomes a design object. Yeohyun Ahn, MFA Studio.

Framing

[The frame] disappears, buries itself, melts away at the moment it deploys its greatest energy. The frame is in no way a background…but neither is its thickness as margin a figure. Or at least it is a figure which comes away of its own accord. Jacques Derrida

Frames are everywhere. A picture frame sets off a work of art from its surroundings, bringing attention to the work and lifting it apart from its setting. Shelves, pedestals, and vitrines provide stages for displaying objects. A saucer frames a tea cup, and a place mat outlines the pieces of a table setting.

Modern designers often seek to eliminate frames. A minimalist interior avoids moldings around doors or woodwork where walls meet the floor, exposing edge-to-edge relationships. The full-bleed photography of a sleek magazine layout eliminates the protective, formal zone of the white margin, allowing the image to explode off the page and into reality.

In politics, "framing" refers to explaining an issue in terms that will influence how people interpret it. The caption of a picture is a frame that guides its interpretation. A billboard is framed by a landscape, and a product is framed by its retail setting. Boundaries and fences mark the frames of private property.

Cropping, borders, margins, and captions are key resources of graphic design. Whether emphasized or erased, frames affect how we perceive information.

Frames create the conditions for understanding an image or object. The philosopher Jacques Derrida defined framing as a structure that is both present and absent.[1] The frame is subservient to the content it surrounds, disappearing as we focus on the image or object on view, and yet the frame shapes our understanding of that content. Frames are part of the fundamental architecture of graphic design. Indeed, framing is one of the most persistent, unavoidable, and infinitely variable acts performed by the graphic designer.

An interface is a kind of frame. The buttons on a television set, the index of a book, or the toolbars of a software application exist outside the central purpose of the product, yet they are essential to our understanding of it. A hammer with no handle or a cell phone with no controls is useless.

Consider the ubiquity of interfaces in the design process. The physical box of the computer screen provides a constant frame for the act of designing, while the digital desktop is edged with controls and littered with icons. Numerous windows compete for our attention, each framed by borders and buttons.

A well-designed interface is both visible and invisible, escaping attention when not needed while shifting into focus on demand. Once learned, interfaces disappear from view, becoming second nature.

Experimental design often exposes or dramatizes the interface: a page number or a field of white space might become a pronounced visual element, or a navigation panel might assume an unusual shape or position. By pushing the frame into the foreground, such acts provoke the discovery of new ideas.

This chapter shows how the meaning and impact of an image or text changes depending on how it is bordered or cropped. Frames typically serve to contain an image, marking it off from its background in order to make it more visible. Framing can also penetrate the image, rendering it open and permeable rather than stable and contained. A frame can divide an image from its background, but it can also serve as a transition from inside to outside, figure to ground.

1. Jacques Derrida, *The Truth in Painting*, trans. Geoff Bennington and Ian McLeod (Chicago: University of Chicago Press, 1987).

Camera Frames

The mechanical eye of the camera cuts up the field of vision in a way that the natural eye does not. Every time you snap a picture with a camera, you make a frame. In contrast, the eye is in constant motion, focusing and refocusing on diverse stimuli in the environment.

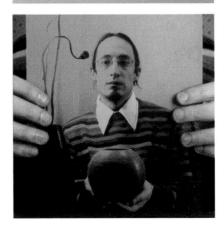

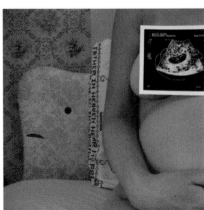

Frames Inside of Frames Frames exist throughout the environment. The photographs shown here use the tool of the camera to create not only the outer frame of the shot, but to discover inner frames as well. Sarah Joy Jordahl Verville, MFA Studio.

Framing and Reframing Here, the artist rephotographed pictures collected from the history and future of his own family in environments that are endowed with both historic and contemporary detail. Jeremy Botts, MFA Studio. Corinne Botz, faculty.

Cropping

By cropping a photograph or illustration, the designer redraws its borders and alters its shape, changing the scale of its elements in relation to the overall picture. A vertical image can become a square, a circle, or a narrow ribbon, acquiring new proportions. By closing in on a detail, cropping can change the focus of a picture, giving it new meaning and emphasis.

By cropping a picture, the designer can discover new images inside it. Experiment with cropping by laying two L-shaped pieces of paper over an image, or look at the picture through a window cut from a piece of paper. Working digitally, move an image around inside the picture frame in a page-layout program, changing its scale, position, and orientation.

New Frame, New Meaning The way an image is cropped can change its meaning completely. Yong Seuk Lee, MFA Studio.

Margin A margin creates a protective zone around an image, presenting it as an object on a stage, a figure against a ground. Margins can be thick or thin, symmetrical or asymmetrical. A wider margin can add formality to the image it frames.

Margins and Bleeds

Margins affect the way we perceive content by providing open spaces around texts and images. Wider margins can emphasize a picture or a field of text as an object, calling our attention to it. Narrower margins can make the content seem larger than life, bursting at its own seams.

Margins provide a protective frame around the contents of a publication. They also provide space for information such as page numbers and running heads. A deep margin can accommodate illustrations, captions, headings, and other information.

Full Bleed An image "bleeds" when it runs off the edges of a page. The ground disappears, and the image seems larger and more active.

Partial Bleed An image can bleed off one, two, or three sides. Here, the bottom margin provides a partial border, yet the photograph still has a larger-than-life quality.

Bleeds The picture above is reproduced at the same scale in each instance, but its intimacy and impact change as it takes over more or less of the surrounding page.

EMPTY SPACE AVAILABLE. COMMERCIAL LEASE, 10,000 SQUARE FT.

Framing Image and Text

An image seen alone, without any words, is open to interpretation. Adding text to a picture changes its meaning. Written language becomes a frame for the image, shaping the viewer's understanding of it both through the content of the words and the style and placement of the typography. Likewise, pictures can change the meaning of a text.

Text and image combine in endless ways. Text can be subordinate or dominant to a picture; it can be large or small, inside or outside, opaque or transparent, legible or obscure. Text can respect or ignore the borders of an image.

From Caption to Headline When a large-scale word replaces an ordinary caption, the message changes. What is empty? The sky, the store, or the larger social reality suggested by the landscape?

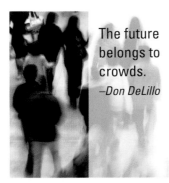

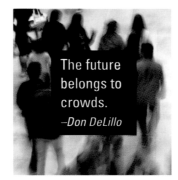

Text Over Image Putting type on top of a high-contrast image poses legibility conflicts. Boxes, bars, and transparent color fields are some of the ways designers deal with the problem of separating text from image.

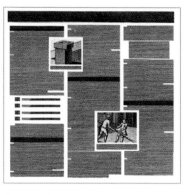

Shannon Snyder

Jessica Alvarado

Melanie M. Rodgers

Lindsay Olson

Using Images Typographically How can an image be arranged, like type, into words, lines, columns, and grids? This exercise invited designers to think abstractly about both image and type. Each designer created a new visual "text" by mining lines, shapes, and textures from a larger picture. Typography is experienced in terms of blocks of graphic tone and texture that are framed by the margins and gutters of the page. Different densities of texture suggest hierarchies of contrasting typefaces. Headlines, captions, quotations, lists, illustrations, and other material take shape in relation to bodies of running text. Advanced Design Workshop, York College. Ellen Lupton, visiting faculty.

The exercises on this spread incorporate a high-resolution scan of an original eighteenth-century engraving from Denis Diderot's *Encyclopedia*. Shown here is the full image.

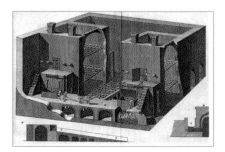

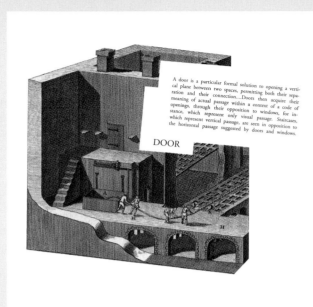

Luke Williams

Jessica Neil

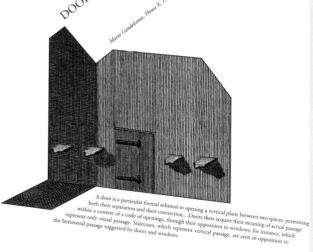

Jonnie Hallman

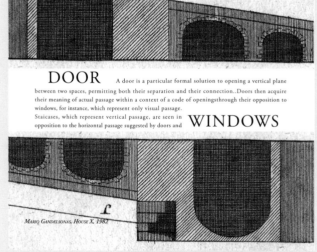

Lindsey Sherman

Framing Text and Image In this project, designers edited, framed, and cropped a picture in relation to a passage of text. The challenge was to make the text an equal player in the final composition, not a mere caption or footnote to the picture.

Designers approached the image abstractly as well as figuratively. Is the picture flat or three-dimensional? How does it look upside down? Designers edited the image by blocking out parts of it, changing the shape of the frame, or blowing up a detail.

They found lines, shapes, and planes within the picture that suggested ways to position and align the text. The goal was to integrate the text with the image without letting the text disappear. Typography I. Ellen Lupton, faculty.

PRODUCT OF TRINIDAD & TOBAGO

OVER 65% ALC./VOL.

Villa Borghese, Rome, 1615. The ornament on this Renaissance palazzo frames the windows, doors, and niches as well as delineates the building's principal volumes and divisions. Architect: Giovanni Vasanzio. Vintage photograph.

Borders

A border is the frontier between inside and outside, marking the edge of a territory. A border naturally appears where an image ends and its background begins.

While many images hold their own edges (a dark picture on a white background), a graphic border can help define an image that lacks an obvious edge (a white background on a white page). A graphic border can emphasize an outer boundary, or it can frame off a section inside an image. Some borders are simple lines; others are detailed and complex. Around the world and across history, people have created elaborate frames, rules, cartouches, and moldings to frame pictures and architectural elements.

Whether simple or decorative, a border creates a transition between image and background. Against the pale wall of a room, for example, a black picture frame sharply separates a work of art from its surroundings. Alternatively, a frame whose color is close to that of the wall blends the work of art with the room around it. Graphic designers make similar decisions when framing visual elements, sometimes seeking to meld them with their context, and sometimes seeking to set them sharply apart. A frame can serve to either emphasize or downplay its contents.

Marking Space A frame can mark off a space with just a few points. Territory can be defined from the outside in (as in crop marks for trimming a print), or from the inside out (an x drawn from the center of a space to its four corners).

Border Patrol Frames interact with content in different ways. In the examples shown here, the border sometimes calls attention to the icon, lending it stature; in other instances, the border itself takes over, becoming the dominant form. Robert Lewis, MFA Studio.

MUSEUM
OF
NOTES

Flexible Museum Identity The shape of
the frame around the museum's name
references folded paper and post-it notes,
and the neon colors are inspired by high-
lighter pens. The frame of the logotype can
be stretched to fit different applications.
Lolo Zhang, MFA Studio.

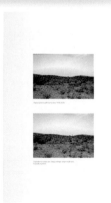

Publication: Page and Screen This
publication has a double structure that is
interpreted differently in print and online.
Alex Jacque, MFA Studio.

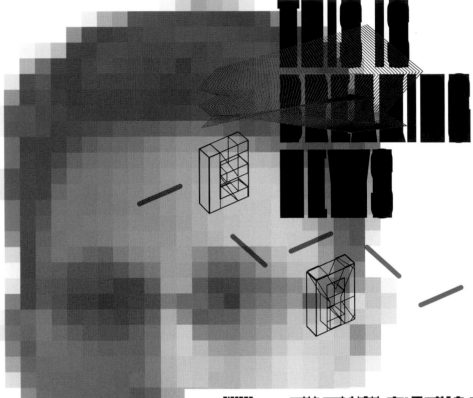

Hierarchy

Design is the conscious effort to impose a **meaningful order**.
Victor Papanek

Hierarchy is the order of importance within a social group (such as the regiments of an army) or in a body of text (such as the sections and subsections of a book). Hierarchical order exists in nearly everything we know, including the family unit, the workplace, politics, and religion. Rankings of power and position define who we are as a culture.

Hierarchy is expressed through naming systems: general, colonel, corporal, private, and so on. Hierarchy is also conveyed visually, through variations in scale, value, color, spacing, placement, and other signals. Expressing order is a central task of the graphic designer. Visual hierarchy controls the delivery and impact of a message. Without hierarchy, graphic communication is dull and difficult to navigate.

Like fashion, graphic design cycles through periods of structure and chaos, ornament and austerity. A designer's approach to visual hierarchy reflects his or her personal style, methodology, and training as well as the zeitgeist of the period. Hierarchy can be simple or complex, rigorous or loose, flat or highly articulated. Regardless of approach, hierarchy employs clear marks of separation to signal a change from one level to another. As in music, the ability to articulate variation in tone, pitch, and melody in design requires careful delineation.

In interaction design, menus, texts, and images can be given visual order through placement and consistent styling, but the user often controls the order in which information is accessed. Unlike a linear book, interactive spaces feature multiple links and navigation options that parcel content according to the user's actions. Cascading Style Sheets (CSS) articulate the structure of a document separately from its presentation so that information can be automatically reconfigured for different output devices, from desktop computer screens to mobile phones, PDAs, kiosks, and more. A slightly different visual hierarchy might be used in each instance.

The average computer desktop supports a complex hierarchy of icons, applications, folders, menus, images, and palettes—empowering users, as never before, to arrange, access, edit, and order vast amounts of information—all managed through a flexible hierarchy controlled and customized by the user.

As technology allows ever greater access to information, the ability of the designer to distill and make sense of the data glut gains increasing value.

Seeing What Matters Even though the designer pixelated and abstracted the content of this simulated newspaper page, visual cues enable readers to understand the basic hierarchy. Chen Zui, MFA Studio.

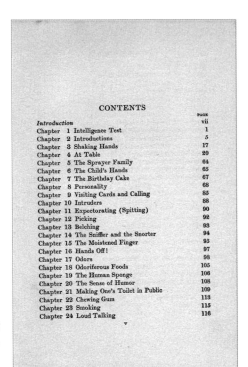

What's Wrong with this Picture?
The function of a table of contents is to list the elements of a book and help readers locate them. In the table of contents shown here, the page numbers are stretched across the page from the chapter titles, and the word "Chapter" has been repeated twenty-four times. *Manners for the Millions*, 1932.

Basic Typographic Hierarchy
The table of contents of a printed book—especially one with many parts—provides a structural picture of the text to follow. When books are marketed online, the table of contents is often reproduced to allow potential buyers to preview the book. A well-designed table of contents is thus not only functional but also visually exciting and memorable.

The basic function of a table of contents is to help readers locate relevant information and provide an image of how the book is organized. Does the text fall into a few main parts with various subdivisions, or does it consist of numerous small, parallel entries? The designer uses alignment, leading, indents, and type sizes and styles to construct a clear and descriptive hierarchy.

A poorly designed table of contents often employs conflicting and contradictory alignments, redundant numbering systems, and a clutter of graphic elements. Analyzing tables of contents— as well as restaurant menus and commercial catalogs—is a valuable exercise.

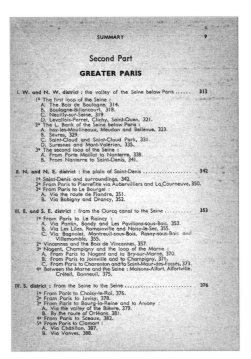

Lost in Paris In this table of contents for a travel guide, the designer has used a muddled mix of centered, justified, and flush-left alignments. The desire to create an overall justified setting dominates the logic of the page—hence the long first lines and rows of dots at the top level of information. The three titling lines at the head of the page are centered (a traditional solution), but the result is awkward in relation to the irregular mass of subheads, which weight the page to the left. The whole affair is further confused by the elaborate system of indents, numerals, and letters used to outline the book's subsections. *Blue Guide to Paris*, 1957.

CONTENTS

EMPIRE

Book as Billboard This table of contents serves as a billboard for the book as well as a functional guide to its elements. The designer has approached the spread as a whole, with content stretching across it horizontally. The page numbers are aligned in columns next to the article titles, making it easy for readers to connect content with location. (No old-fashioned leader lines needed!) Chapter numbers aren't necessary because the sequential page numbers are sufficient to indicate the order of the pieces. The book has many contributors, a point made clear through the type styling. Nicholas Blechman, *Empire*, 2004.

Think with the Senses
Feel with the Mind.
Art in the Present Tense
Venice Biennale
52nd International Art Exhibition
10 June – 21 November
National and Regional Pavilions
and Presentations.
Parallel Exhibitions and Projects

No hierarchy

Think with the Senses
Feel with the Mind.
Art in the Present Tense
Venice Biennale
52nd International Art Exhibition
10 June – 21 November
National and Regional Pavilions
and Presentations.
Parallel Exhibitions and Projects

Contrasting weight

Think with the Senses
Feel with the Mind.
Art in the Present Tense
Venice Biennale
52nd International Art Exhibition
10 June – 21 November
National and Regional Pavilions
and Presentations.
Parallel Exhibitions and Projects

Contrasting color

Think with the Senses
Feel with the Mind.
Art in the Present Tense
Venice Biennale
52nd International Art Exhibition
10 June – 21 November
National and Regional Pavilions
and Presentations.
Parallel Exhibitions and Projects

Alignment

Think with the Senses
Feel with the Mind.
Art in the Present Tense

Venice Biennale

52nd International Art Exhibition
10 June – 21 November
National and Regional Pavilions
and Presentations.
Parallel Exhibitions and Projects

Spatial intervals

Think with the Senses
Feel with the Mind.
Art in the Present Tense

VENICE BIENNALE

52nd International Art Exhibition
10 June – 21 November

National and Regional Pavilions
and Presentations.
Parallel Exhibitions and Projects

Uppercase and spatial intervals

Think with the Senses
Feel with the Mind.
Art in the Present Tense

Venice Biennale

52nd International Art Exhibition
10 June – 21 November

National and Regional Pavilions
and Presentations.
Parallel Exhibitions and Projects

Weight, color, space, alignment

Think with the Senses
Feel with the Mind.
Art in the Present Tense

Venice Biennale

52nd International Art Exhibition
10 June – 21 November

National and Regional Pavilions
and Presentations.
Parallel Exhibitions and Projects

Scale, space, alignment

Think with the Senses
Feel with the Mind.
Art in the Present Tense

Venice Biennale

52nd International Art Exhibition
10 June – 21 November

National and Regional Pavilions
and Presentations.
Parallel Exhibitions and Projects

Italic, scale, color, alignment

Hierarchy 101 A classic exercise is to work with a basic chunk of information and explore numerous simple variations, using just one type family. The parts of a typographic hierarchy can be signaled with one or more cues: line break, type style, type size, rules, and so on.

HyunSoo Lim
Katie MacLachlan

Claire Smalley
Anna Eshelman

Menu of Options Designers use scale, placement, alignment, type style, and other cues to bring visual order to a body of content. Expressing hierarchy is an active, inquisitive process that can yield dynamic visual results. Typography I. Jennifer Cole Phillips, faculty.

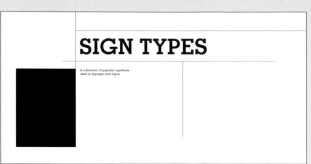

SIGN TYPES

A collection of popular typefaces used in signage and logos.

1929

MEMPHIS

Futura with serifs.

Aa Bb Cc Dd Ee Ff Gg
Hh Ii Jj Kk Ll Mm Nn
Oo Pp Qq Rr Ss Tt Uu
Vv Ww Xx Yy Zz
1 2 3 4 5 6 7 8 9

GATORADE
Polaroid

Designed by the legendary Rudolph Wolf, the Memphis font family was one of the **most popular display fonts** of its time. Often referred to as "Futura with serifs" and named after the ancient Egyptian capital of Memphis, this slab serif was the first modern Egyptian of its time and paved the way for many other slab serif revivals to come.

● ○ ○ ○ ○

1957

HELVETICA

Virtually everything.

Aa Bb Cc Dd Ee Ff Gg
Hh Ii Jj Kk Ll Mm Nn
Oo Pp Qq Rr Ss Tt Uu
Vv Ww Xx Yy Zz
1 2 3 4 5 6 7 8 9

New York City Subway
TOYOTA
THE NORTH FACE
TARGET
American Apparel
Jeep

Helvetica is one of the **most popular** and **widely used typefaces** ever created and continues to be one of the most sought after and frequently specified sans-serifs. It has clean lines, neutrality and great clarity that make it perfect for a wide variety of applications such as corporate identity, newspapers, signage and advertising.

○ ● ○ ○ ○

2000

GOTHAM

Building lettering.

Aa Bb Cc Dd Ee Ff Gg
Hh Ii Jj Kk Ll Mm Nn Oo
Pp Qq Rr Ss Tt Uu Vv
Ww Xx Yy Zz
1 2 3 4 5 6 7 8 9

Obama's 2008 campaign
GQ Magazine
One World Trade Center
Discovery Channel
HGTV Channel
Rite Aid Pharmacy

Gotham is a frequently used **geometric** san serif. It was designed by American type designer Tobias Frere-Jones in 2002. Gotham's letterforms are inspired by a form of **architectural** signage that became popular in the 20th century. It is especially popular throughout NYC.

○ ○ ● ○ ○

1845

CLARENDON

First registered typeface.

Aa Bb Cc Dd Ee Ff
Gg Hh Ii Jj Kk Ll
Mm Nn Oo Pp Qq
Rr Ss Tt Uu Vv Ww
Xx Yy Zz
1 2 3 4 5 6 7 8 9

US National Park Signs
Tonka Truck Brand
Great Western Railway
WELLS FARGO logo
Numbers on Wheel of Fortune

Clarendon was first designed to "serve as a **display letter** in a mass of text-type, and also for side headings in many dictionaries and reference books." It is an English slab-serif typeface that was created in England by Robert Besley in 1845. He tried to patent the typeface, as Clarendon is now known as the first registered typeface. When it became popular it was copied by other foundries. It established the use of **bold face** to pick out parts of the text.

○ ○ ○ ● ○

1931

DIN

German traffic signage.

Aa Bb Cc Dd Ee Ff Gg
Hh Ii Jj Kk Ll Mm Nn
Oo Pp Qq Rr Ss Tt Uu
Vv Ww Xx Yy Zz
1 2 3 4 5 6 7 8 9

Autobahn German Signage
iphone iOS 7 Camera App
THE WOLF OF WALL STREET

DIN 1451 standard is a commonly used default font for traffic signs. It is also used in street signs and house numbers, and until 2000, it was used for German license plates. In 1995, type designer Albert-Jan Pool expanded DIN 1451 into a more polished form used most often in graphic design and publishing. It is referred to as FF DIN.

○ ○ ○ ○ ●

Melissa Hecker

Typeface Specimen Book
Graphic Design 1
May 2014

Five Fonts In this twist on the classic type specimen book, designers curate a collection of five typefaces and design a typographic hierarchy. Key content includes the typeface name, designer, year created, and descriptive or historical text. The compositional landscapes also contain a character set and some visual element focusing attention on the typeface's expressive or formal qualities. In structuring multiple pages, students consider continuity and pacing. Covers and colophons become graceful extensions of the interior. Typography I. Jennifer Cole Phillips, faculty.

Melissa Hecker

Eames
A House Industries Font Family

Century Modern

THIN ITALIC

"The *details* are not the details. They make the product."

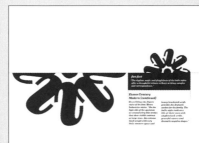
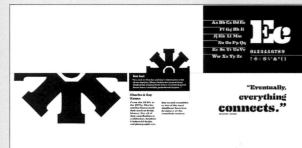

the knowledge enrich feelings

REGULAR

"Eventually, everything connects."

STENCIL

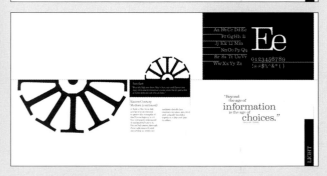

"Take your pleasure seriously."

BOLD ITALIC

"Beyond the age of information is the age of choices."

LIGHT

Theresa Bonaddio

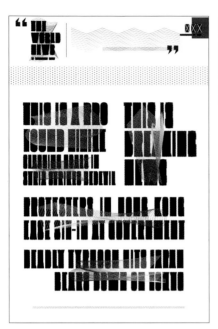

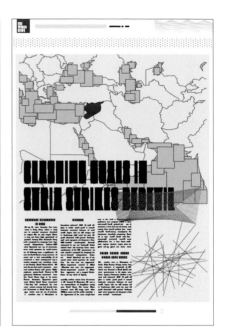

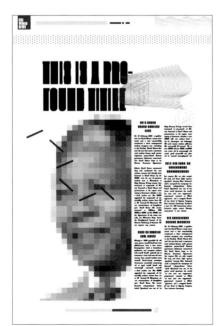

Content Vacuum In this project the designer purposefully abstracted the content of newspaper pages, thereby drawing attention to the visual hierarchy. Chen Zui, MFA Studio.

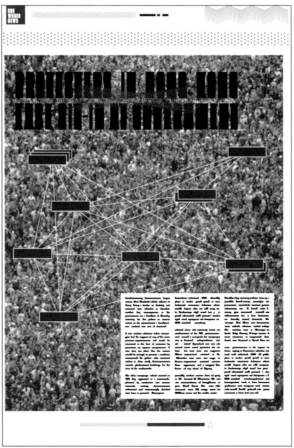

Content Glut This program for an arts festival contains multiple levels of typographic and photographic information, requiring the designer to establish clear and consistent visual signals of separation across all hierarchical levels. Amy Hushen, Advanced Graphic Design. Jennifer Cole Phillips, faculty.

Inverted Hierarchy The designer has placed suggestions for food compatibility at the top of the hierarchy on these spice bottles, subordinating the product name. Amy Lee Walton, Post Baccalaureate Workshop.

Dimensional Hierarchy
Messages applied to three-dimensional form have the added challenge of legibility across and around planes. Objects sitting in an environment are bathed in shadow and light. Unlike books that can conceal elaborate worlds inside their covers—automatically separated from exterior contexts—environmental messages must interact beyond their boundaries and become either a harmonious or poignant counterpoint to their neighbors.

Notice in these examples how type, color fields, and graphic elements carry the viewer's eye around the dimensional form, often making a visual if not verbal connection with neighboring packages when stacked side by side or vertically.

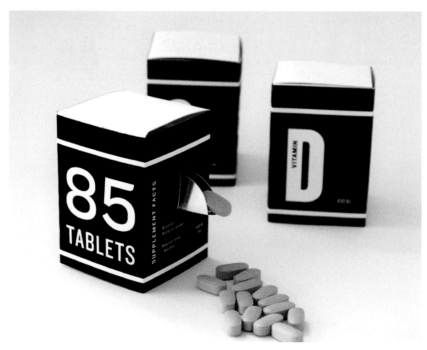

Dynamic Dosage A visual hierarchy is often necessary for objects in a series. This bold design for vitamin packaging magnifies unexpected product details and provides a surprising spout for dispensing tablets. James Anderson, Typography II. Jennifer Cole Phillips, faculty

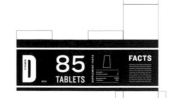

Architecture of Snacks This design series for iconic snacks discards the usual overt cacophony of branding language in favor of a clear, stripped-down information hierarchy that situates the brand name neutrally with typography that sits back, while the celebrated ingredient takes center stage in exploded axonometric renderings. James Anderson, Advanced Graphic Design. Jennifer Cole Phillips, faculty

Going with the Flow The designer has built a visual language for a line of tampons that elevates the aesthetics for a more welcome place in the medicine cabinet. Visual pattern density signifies relative absorbency. Heda Hokschirr, Advanced Graphic Design. Jennifer Cole Phillips, faculty

Layers

Under cities you always find **other cities**; under churches other churches; and under houses other houses. Pablo Picasso

Layers are simultaneous, overlapping components of an image or sequence. They are at work in countless media software programs, from Photoshop and Illustrator to audio, video, and animation tools, where multiple layers of image and sound (tracks) unfold in time.

The concept of layers comes from the physical world, and it has a long history in the traditions of mapping and musical notation. Maps and time lines use overlapping layers to associate different levels of data, allowing them to contribute to the whole while maintaining their own identities.

Most printing techniques require that an image be split into layers before it can be reproduced. From ink-jet printing to silkscreen and commercial lithography, each color requires its own plate, film, screen, ink cartridge, or toner drum, depending on the process. Digital technologies automate this process, making it more or less invisible to the designer.

Before the early 1990s, designers created "mechanicals" consisting of precisely aligned layers of paper and acetate. The designer or paste-up artist adhered each element of the page—type, images, blocks of color—to a separate layer, placing any element that touches any other element on its own surface.

This same principle is at work in the digital layers we use today, mobilized in new and powerful ways. The layers feature in Photoshop creates a new layer whenever the user adds text or pastes an image. Each layer can be independently filtered, transformed, masked, or multiplied. Adjustment layers allow global changes such as levels and curves to be revised or discarded at any time. The image file becomes an archaeology of its own making, a stack of elements seen simultaneously in the main window, but represented as a vertical list in the layers palette.

Layers allow the designer to treat the image as a collection of assets, a database of possibilities. Working with a layered file, the designer quickly creates variations of a single design by turning layers on and off. Designers use layered files to generate storyboards for animations and interface elements such as buttons and rollovers.

Although the layered archeology of the printed page or digital file tends to disappear in the final piece, experimental work often uncovers visual possibilities by exposing layers. The Dutch designer Jan van Toorn has used cut-and-paste techniques to create images whose complex surfaces suggest political action and unrest.

Many designers have explored an off-register or misprinted look, seeking rawness and accidental effects by exposing the layers of the printing and production processes. Contemporary graphic artists Ryan McGinness and Joshua Davis create graphic images composed of enormous numbers of layers that overlap in arbitrary, seemingly uncoordinated ways.

Layers, always embedded in the process of mechanical reproduction, have become intuitive and universal. They are crucial to how we both read and produce graphic images today.

Printed Layers Artist and designer Ryan McGinness piles numerous layers on top of each other to yield composite images that celebrate both flatness and depth. Ryan McGinness, *Arab Cadillac Generator*, 2006. Acrylic on wood panel, 48 inches diameter. Collection of Charles Saatchi. Courtesy Deitch Projects, New York. Photo: Tom Powel Imaging, Inc.

Cut and Paste

The cubist painters popularized collage in the early twentieth century. By combining bits of printed paper with their own drawn and painted surfaces, they created an artistic technique that profoundly influenced both design and the fine arts. Like the cubists, modern graphic designers use collage to juxtapose layers of content, yielding surfaces that oscillate between flatness and depth, positive and negative.

The cut-and-paste function used in nearly every software application today refers to the physical process of collage. Each time you copy or delete a picture or phrase and insert it into a new position, you reference the material act of cutting and pasting. The collaged history of an image or a document largely disappears in the final work, and designers often strive to create seamless, invisible transitions between elements. Foregrounding the cut-and-paste process can yield powerful results that indicate the designer's role in shaping meaning.

Mixing Media Published in 1989 to commemorate the Declaration of Human Rights a century earlier, this poster by Jan van Toorn used photomechanical processes to mix handmade and mass-media imagery. Scraps of paper radiate like energy from the central handshake. Jan van Toorn, *La Lutte Continue* (The Fight Continues), 1989.

Cut, Paste, Tape, Splice These posters originated from hands-on experiments with physical cutting and pasting, which then evolved into digital interpretations. Luke Williams, Graphic Design I. Bernard Canniffe, faculty.

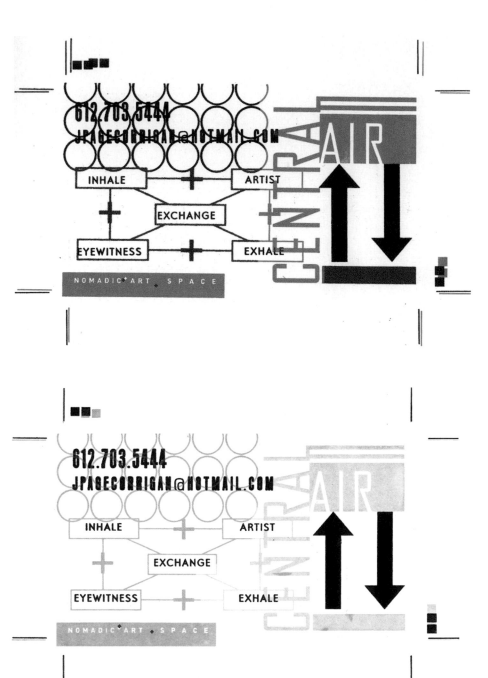

Printed Layers Nearly every color printing process uses layers of ink, but the layers are usually compiled to create the appearance of a seamless, singular surface. The screen prints above use overlapping and misaligned layers of ink to call attention to the structure of the surface. John P. Corrigan, MFA Studio.

Makeready To conserve materials, printers reuse old press sheets while getting their presses up to speed, testing ink flow and position before pulling their final prints. Called "makereadies," these layered surfaces are full of beautiful accidental effects, as seen in this screen-printed makeready. Paul Sahre and David Plunkert.

SEPTEMBER 27 THRU OCTOBER 27
DIRECTED BY SUSAN KRAMER
BALTIMORE PREMIERE!
A PLAY BY: JON KLEIN
BY: WALLACE
PERFORMED BY: NEAL

HyunSoo Lim

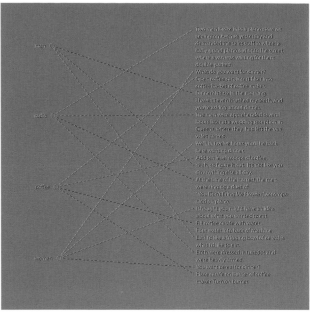

April Osmanof

Typographic Layers In everyday life as well as in films and animations, multiple stories can unfold simultaneously. A person can talk on the phone while folding the laundry and hearing a song in the background. In films, characters often carry on a conversation while performing an action.

This typographic exercise presents three narratives taking place during a two-minute period: a news story broadcast on a radio, a conversation between a married couple, and the preparation of a pot of coffee. Typography, icons, lines, and other elements are used to present the three narratives within a shared space. The end result can be obvious or poetic. Whether the final piece is an easy-to-follow transcription or a painterly depiction, it is made up of narrative elements that define distinct layers or visual channels. Graphic Design MFA Studio.

Yong Seuk Lee

Temporal Layers This publication records a collaboration between two universities in China and Russia. The large-scale numerals reference numbers in a calendar. Overlapping forms, images, and text blocks suggest depth and motion. Li Shaobo and Wenjie Lu.

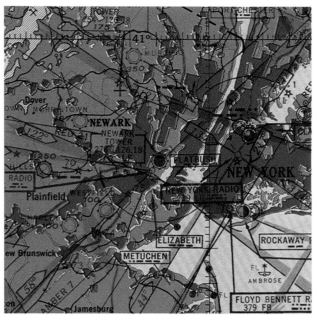

Data Layers: Static This map uses point, line, plane, and color to indicate geographic borders, topographical features, towns and cities, and points of interest, as well as radio systems used by pilots in the air. The purple lines indicating radio signals read as a separate layer. Aeronautical map, 1946.

Data Layers

Maps compress various types of information—topography, water systems, roadways, cities, geographic borders, and so on—onto a single surface. Map designers use color, line, texture, symbols, icons, and typography to create different levels of information, allowing users to read levels independently (for example, learning what roads connect two destinations) as well as perceiving connections between levels (will the journey be mountainous or flat?).

Sophisticated map-making tools are now accessible to designers and general practitioners as well as to professional cartographers. Google Earth enables users to build personalized maps using satellite photography of the Earth's surface. The ability to layer information over a base image is a central feature of this immensely powerful yet widely available tool.

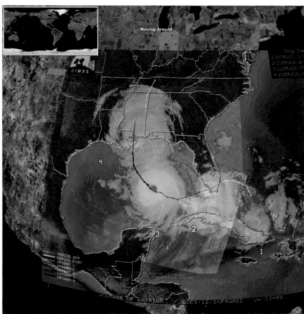

Data Layers: Dynamic An image of Hurricane Katrina has been layered over a satellite photograph of Earth. The end user of a Google Earth overlay can manipulate its transparency in order to control the degree of separation between the added layer and the ground image. Storm: University of Wisconsin, Madison Cooperative Institute for Meteorological Satellite Studies, 2005. Composite: Jack Gondela.

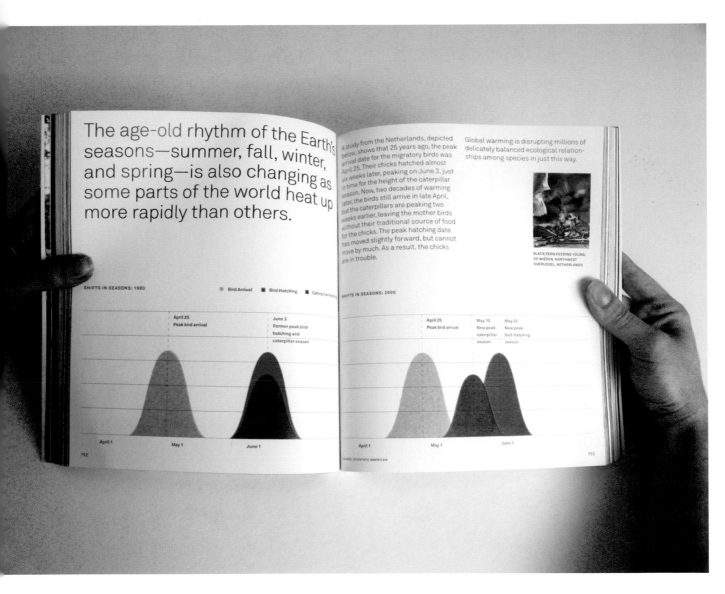

The age-old rhythm of the Earth's seasons—summer, fall, winter, and spring—is also changing as some parts of the world heat up more rapidly than others.

A study from the Netherlands, depicted below, shows that 25 years ago, the peak arrival date for the migratory birds was April 25. Their chicks hatched almost six weeks later, peaking on June 3, just in time for the height of the caterpillar season. Now, two decades of warming later, the birds still arrive in late April, but the caterpillars are peaking two weeks earlier, leaving the mother birds without their traditional source of food for the chicks. The peak hatching date has moved slightly forward, but cannot move by much. As a result, the chicks are in trouble.

Global warming is disrupting millions of delicately balanced ecological relationships among species in just this way.

BLACK TERN FEEDING YOUNG, DE WIEDEN, NORTHWEST OVERIJSSEL, NETHERLANDS

SHIFTS IN SEASONS: 1980

Bird Arrival   Bird Hatching   Caterpillar

April 25
Peak bird arrival

June 3
Former peak bird-hatching and caterpillar season

April 1   May 1   June 1

152

SHIFTS IN SEASONS: 2000

April 25
Peak bird arrival

May 15
New peak caterpillar season

May 25
New peak bird-hatching season

April 1   May 1   June 1

SOURCE: SCIENTIFIC AMERICAN

153

Comparing Data Layers In this graph from Al Gore's book *An Inconvenient Truth,* the designers have used color and transparency to make it easy for readers to compare two sets of data. The graphs show how climate change is affecting the life cycle of animals and their food supplies. Alicia Cheng, Stephanie Church, and Lisa Maione, MGMT Design, *An Inconvenient Truth*, 2006.

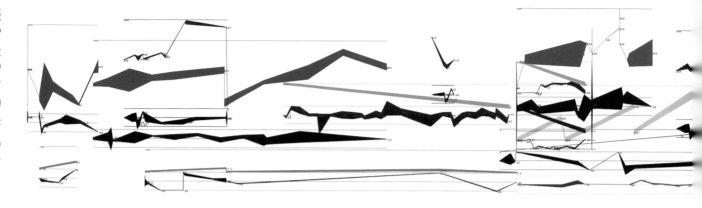

Musical Notation This score shows the notes played by four different musicians simultaneously (first violin, second violin, viola, and cello). Each staff represents a separate instrument. Ludwig van Beethoven, musical score, *String Quartet No. 2 in G Major*, 1799.

Temporal Layers

In musical notation, the notes for each instrument in a symphony or for each voice in a chorus appear on parallel staffs. The graphic timelines used in audio, video, and animation software follow this intuitive convention, using simultaneous tracks to create composite layers of image and sound.

In soap operas and television dramas, parallel threads unfold alongside each other and converge at key moments in the story. The split screens, inset panels, and text feeds commonly seen in news programming allow several visual tracks to play simultaneously.

From musical notation and computer interfaces to narrative plot lines, parallel linear tracks (layers in time) are a crucial means for describing simultaneous events.

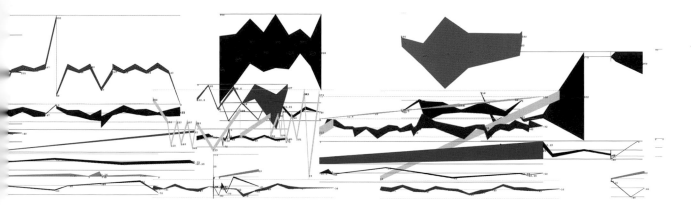

Interactive Notation Digital composer Hans-Christoph Steiner has devised his own graphic notation system to show how to manipulate digital samples. Time flows from left to right. Each color represents a sample.

Each sample controller has two arrays: the brighter, bigger one on top controls sample playback, and a smaller, darker one at the bottom controls amp and pan. The lowest point of the sample array is the beginning

of the sample, the highest is the end, and the height of the array is how much and what part of the sample to play, starting at that point in time. Hans-Christoph Steiner, interactive musical score, *Solitude*, 2004.

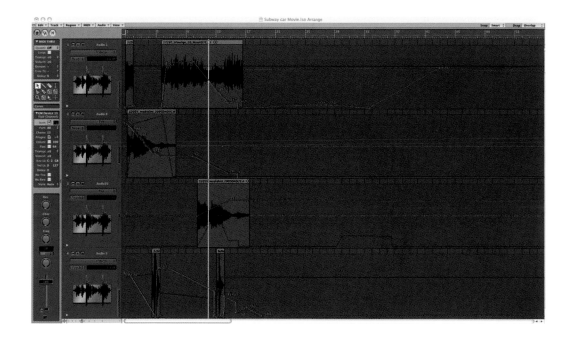

Audio Software Applications for editing digital audio tracks employ complex and varied graphics. Here, each track is represented by a separate timeline. The yellow lines indicate volume, and the green lines show panning left to right. Audio composed by Jason Okutake, MFA Studio. Software: Apple Logic Pro Audio.

Lauretta Dolch

Physical, Virtual, and Temporal Layers In this project, designers began by creating a series of six-by-six-inch collages with four square sheets of colored paper. (We used origami paper). Each designer cut a square window into a larger sheet of paper so that they could move the colored sheets around and experiment with different designs.

In the second phase of the project, designers translated one of their physical collages into digital layers. Each physical layer became a separate layer in the digital file. They generated new compositions by digitally changing the color, scale, transparency, orientation, and position of the digital layers.

In the third phase, one digital composition became a style frame (the basis of a sequential animation). Each designer planned a sequence, approximately ten seconds long, that loops: that is, it begins and ends on an identical frame. They created nine-panel storyboards showing the sequence.

In the final phase, designers imported their style frames into a digital animation program (Flash), distributing each layer of the style frame to a layer in the timeline to create strata that change over time. Graphic Design II. Ellen Lupton, faculty.

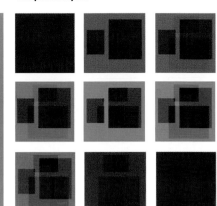

Windows Each layer is a window through which other layers are visible. Kelly Horigan.

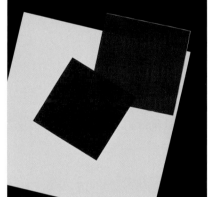

Squares Complete, uncut squares move in and out of the frame. Doug Hucker.

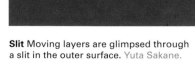

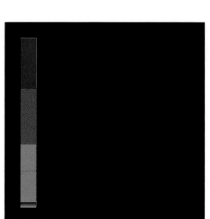

Slit Moving layers are glimpsed through a slit in the outer surface. Yuta Sakane.

© 2006 Europa Tec
Image © 2006 Terr

Transparency

Transparency means a **simultaneous perception of different spatial locations**....The position of the transparent figures has equivocal meaning as one sees each figure now as the closer, now as the farther one. Gyorgy Kepes

As a social value, transparency suggests clarity and directness. The idea of "transparent government" promotes processes that are open and understandable to the public, not hidden behind closed doors. Yet in design, transparency is often used not for the purposes of clarity, but to create dense, layered imagery built from veils of color and texture.

Any surface in the physical world is more or less transparent or opaque: a piece of wood has 100 percent opacity, while a room full of air has nearly zero. Image-editing software allows designers to adjust the opacity of any still or moving picture. Software lets you see through wood, or make air into a solid wall.

Transparency becomes an active design element when its value is somewhere between zero and 100 percent. In this chapter, we assume that a "transparent" image or surface is, generally, opaque to some degree. Indeed, you will discover that a surface built out of completely opaque elements can function in a transparent way.

Transparency and layers are related phenomena. A transparent square of color appears merely pale or faded until it passes over another shape or surface, allowing a second image to show through itself. A viewer thus perceives the transparency of one plane in relation to a second one. What is in front, and what is behind? What dominates, and what recedes?

Video and animation programs allow transparency to change over time. A fade is created by making a clip gradually become transparent. Dissolves occur when one clip fades out (becoming transparent) while a second clip fades in (becoming opaque).

This chapter begins by observing the properties of physical transparency, and then shows how to build transparent surfaces out of opaque graphic elements. We conclude by looking at the infinite malleability of digital transparency.

Transparency is a fascinating and seductive principle. How can it be used to build meaningful images? Transparency can serve to emphasize values of directness and clarity through adjustments and juxtapositions that maintain the wholeness or legibility of elements. Transparency also can serve to build complexity by allowing layers to mix and merge together. Transparency can be used thematically to combine or contrast ideas, linking levels of content. When used in a conscious and deliberate way, transparency contributes to the meaning and visual intrigue of a work of design.

Life History Historical and contemporary photographs and documents are layered over a satellite image from Google Earth of the land these people have inhabited. Transparency is used to separate the elements visually. Jeremy Botts, MFA Studio.

Water Jason Okutake

Physical Transparency

No material is wholly transparent. Ripples disturb the transparency of water, while air becomes thick with smoke or haze. Glass can be tinted, mirrored, cracked, etched, scratched, frosted, or painted to diminish its transparency. The reflective character of glass makes it partially opaque, an attribute that changes depending on light conditions.

A solid material such as wood or metal becomes transparent when its surface is perforated or interrupted. Venetian blinds shift from opaque to transparent as the slats slant open. Adjusting the blinds changes their degree of transparency.

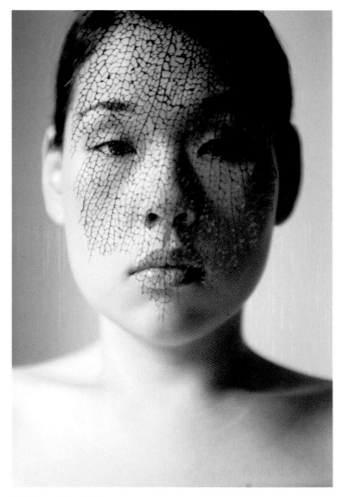

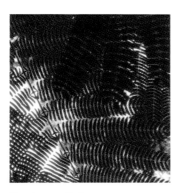

Tree Jeremy Botts

Veil Nancy Froehlich

Ribbon Yue Tuo

Materials and Substances Observing
transparent objects and surfaces throughout
the physical environment yields countless
ideas for combining images and surfaces in
two-dimensional design. MFA Studio.

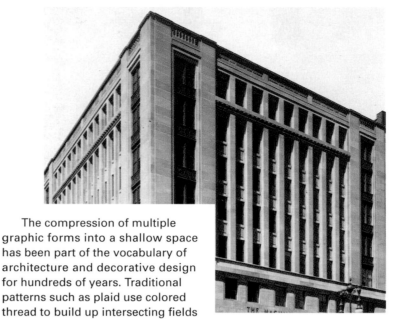

Macmillan Company Building, New York, 1924. This early skyscraper employs vertical elements that span the upper stories of the building. The horizontal elements sit back behind the vertical surface, establishing a second plane that appears to pass continuously behind the front plane, like the threads in a plaid fabric. Architects: Carrère and Hastings with Shreve and Lamb. Vintage photograph.

Graphic Transparency

Designers can translate the effects of physical transparency into overlapping layers of lines, shapes, textures, or letterforms. We call this phenomenon "graphic transparency." Just as in physical transparency, two or more surfaces are visible simultaneously, collapsed onto a single surface. A field of text placed over an image is transparent, revealing parts of the image through its open spaces.

The compression of multiple graphic forms into a shallow space has been part of the vocabulary of architecture and decorative design for hundreds of years. Traditional patterns such as plaid use colored thread to build up intersecting fields of color. Linear elements in classical and modern architecture, such as columns and moldings, often appear to pass through each other.[1]

1. On transparency in architecture, see Colin Rowe and Robert Slutzky, "Transparency: Literal and Phenomenal (Part 2)," in Joan Ockman, ed., *Architecture Culture, 1943–1968: A Documentary Anthology* (New York: Rizzoli, 1993), 205–25.

Plaid Fabric Traditional plaid fabrics are made by weaving together bands of colored thread over and under each other. Where contrasting colors mix, a new color appears. The horizontal and vertical stripes literally pass through each other on the same plane. Lee Jofa, *Carousel*, plaid fabric, cotton and rayon.

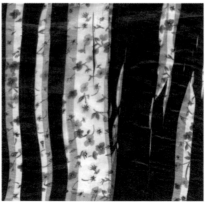

Over-Dyed Fabric To create this non-traditional print, fashion designer Han Feng bunched and folded a delicate floral print and then dyed it, creating long irregular stripes that sit on top of the floral pattern. The result is two competing planes of imagery compressed onto a single surface. Han Feng, polyester fabric.

If one sees two or more figures partly overlapping one another, and each of them claims for itself the **common overlapped part,** then one is confronted with a contradiction of spatial dimensions.

Typographic Plaid Layers of lines pass in front of a base text. The lines are like a slatted or perforated surface through which the text remains visible. Alissa Faden, MFA Studio.

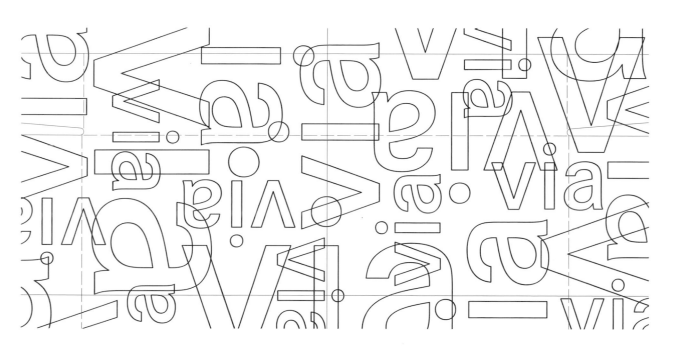

Linear Transparency The letterforms in this pattern have been reduced to outlines, rendering them functionally transparent even as they overlap each other. Abbott Miller and Jeremy Hoffman, Pentagram, packaging for Mohawk Paper.

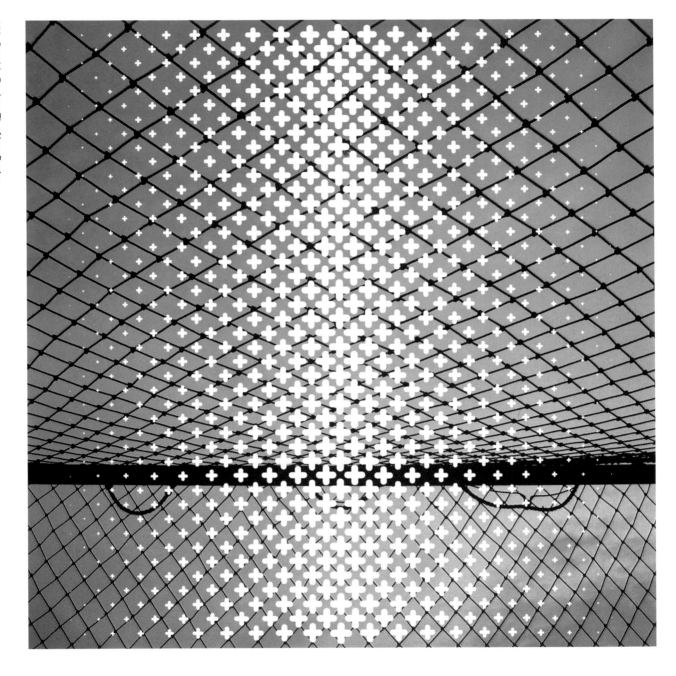

Graphic Transparency In each of these compositions, a photograph has been overlaid with a field of graphic elements. The graphic layer becomes an abstracted commentary on the image underneath. MFA Studio.

Jeremy Botts

Jason Okutake

100 percent opacity

50 percent opacity. Fade-to-black is a standard transition in film and video.

Digital Transparency

Imaging software allows designers to alter the opacity of nearly any graphic element, including type, photographs, and moving images. To do this, the software employs an algorithm that multiplies the tonal values of one layer against those of another, generating a mix between the two layers. To make any image transparent involves compromising its intensity, lowering its overall contrast.

Transparency is used not only to mix two visual elements, but also to make one image fade out against its background. In video and animation, such fades occur over time. The most common technique is the fade-to-black, which employs the default black background. The resulting clip gradually loses intensity while becoming darker. Video editors create a fade-to-white by placing a white background behind the clip. The same effects are used in print graphics to change the relationship between an image and its background.

Transparent type, opaque image

Transparency in type and image

Opposites Attract Transparency serves
to build relationships between images.
Here, male and female mix and overlap.
Jason Okutake, MFA Studio.

Life Lines Transparent layers of text and image
intersect. Kelley McIntyre, MFA Studio.

Wall Flowers Transparent layers build
up to make a dense frame or cartouche.
Jeremy Botts, MFA Studio.

Seeing Through This composition builds relationships between layers of graphic elements and an underlying photograph. The designer has manipulated the elements graphically as well as changing their digital transparency. Yue Tuo, MFA Studio. Photography: Nancy Froehlich.

Modularity

Two eight-stud LEGO bricks can be combined in twenty-four ways.
Three eight-stud LEGO bricks can be combined in 1,060 ways.
Six eight-stud LEGO bricks can be combined in 102,981,500 ways.
With eight bricks the possibilities are virtually endless.

The Ultimate LEGO Book

Every design problem is completed within a set of constraints or limitations. These limits can be as broad as "design a logo," as generic as "print on standard letter paper," or as narrow as "arrange six circles in a square space." Working within the constraints of a problem is part of the fun and challenge of design.

Modularity is a special kind of constraint. A module is a fixed element used within a larger system or structure. For example, a pixel is a module that builds a digital image. A pixel is so small, we rarely stop to notice it, but when designers create pixel-based typefaces, they use a grid of pixels to invent letterforms that are consistent from one to the next while giving each one a distinctive shape.

A nine-by-nine grid of pixels can yield an infinite number of different typefaces. Likewise, a tiny handful of LEGO bricks contains an astonishing number of possible combinations.[1] The endless variety of forms occurs, however, within the strict parameters of the system, which permits just one basic kind of connection.

Building materials—from bricks to lumber to plumbing parts— are manufactured in standard sizes. By working with ready-made materials, an architect helps control construction costs while also streamlining the design process.

Designers are constantly making decisions about size, color, placement, proportion, relationships, and materials as well as about subject matter, style, and imagery. Sometimes, the decision-making process can be so overwhelming, it's hard to know how to begin and when to stop. When a few factors are determined in advance, the designer is free to think about other parts of the problem. A well-defined constraint can free up the thought process by taking some decisions off the table. In creating a page of typography, for example, a designer can choose to work within the constraints of one or two type families, and then explore different combinations of size, weight, and placement within that family of elements.

The book you are reading is organized around a typographic grid whose basic module is a square. By accepting the square unit as a given, we were able to mix and match images while creating a feeling of continuity across the book. The square units vary in size, however (keeping the layouts from getting dull), and some pictures stretch across more than one module (or ignore the grid altogether). Rules are helpful, but it's fun to break them.

Post-it Wallpaper This wall installation was built solely from three colors of Post-it neon note sheets, creating the optical effect of an enlarged halftone image or modular supergraphic. Nolen Strals and Bruce Willen, Post Typography.

1. *The Ultimate LEGO Book* (New York: DK Publishing, 1999).

Alphabet Blocks These rectangular wooden blocks have a different alphabet painted on each side. Nolen Strals and Bruce Willen, Post Typography.

Working with Constraints

In the projects shown here, graphic designers have used modular elements to produce unpredictable results. Try looking at familiar systems from a fresh angle. Given the constraints of any system, how can you play with the rules to make something new?

A child's set of alphabet blocks looks a certain way, for example, because the blocks are made from perfect cubes. But what if alphabet blocks were made from rectangles instead of cubes? The oddly proportioned faces of the blocks at left provided a framework for designing new letterforms in response to the constraints provided by the blocks of wood.

Standard materials such as laser paper are often used in generic ways. A standard sheet of office paper can be very dull indeed. Yet with creative thinking, an ordinary piece of paper can be used for dramatic effect. The temporary signage program shown on the opposite page employs economical processes and everyday materials to produce graphics at a lavish scale— at a very low cost.

Stedlijk Museum CS Signage System This sign system was created for the temporary headquarters of a major museum in the Netherlands. The basic module is a plastic document holder, into which standard sheets of A4 letter paper are inserted. Large-scale graphics are tiled across multiple plastic envelopes. Experimental Jetset.

Kristen Bennett

Clean and Dirty Systems Working with a nine-by-nine-square grid of circles, students created four letterforms with common characteristics such as weight, proportion, and density. Designers then introduced decay, degradation, distortion, randomness, or physicality into the design. The underlying structure becomes an armature for new and unexpected processes.

Designers employed digital techniques, such as applying a filter to the source image or systematically varying the elements, as well as using physical processes such as painting, stitching, or assembling. Typography I. Ellen Lupton, faculty.

Emily Goldfarb

Nicolette Cornelius

Austin Roesberg

Andy Bonner

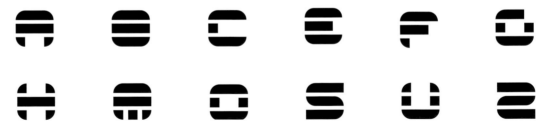

Zachary Richter

Modular Alphabet In these examples, designers created systems of characters using three basic shapes: a square (each side equals one unit), a rectangle (one unit by two units), and a quarter-circle (radius equals one unit). Shapes could be assembled in any way, but their relative scale could not change.

Some forms are dense and solid, while others are split apart. Some use the curved elements to shape the outer edge, while others use curves to cut away the interior. Most have a simple profile, but it is also possible to build a detailed texture out of smaller-scaled elements. Experimental Typography. Nolen Strals and Bruce Willen, faculty.

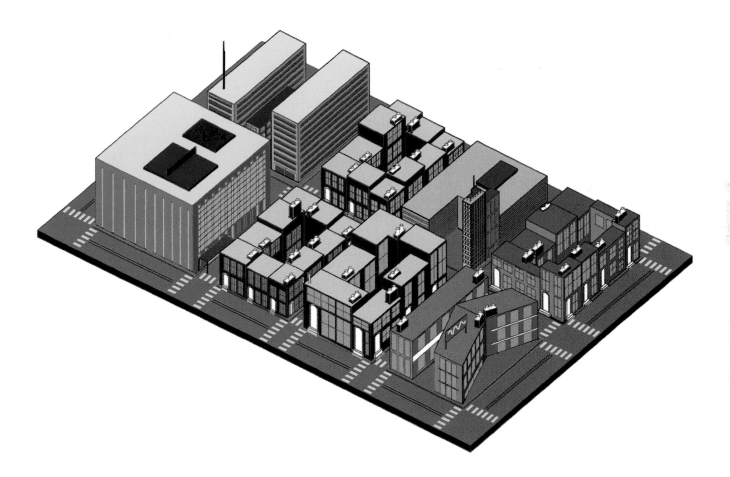

Architectural Alphabet The three-dimensional design software AutoCAD has been used to spell out the phrase "word book" in buildings. The rectilinear modules of architecture become the building blocks for letterforms. Johanna Barthmaier, Typography I. Ellen Lupton, faculty.

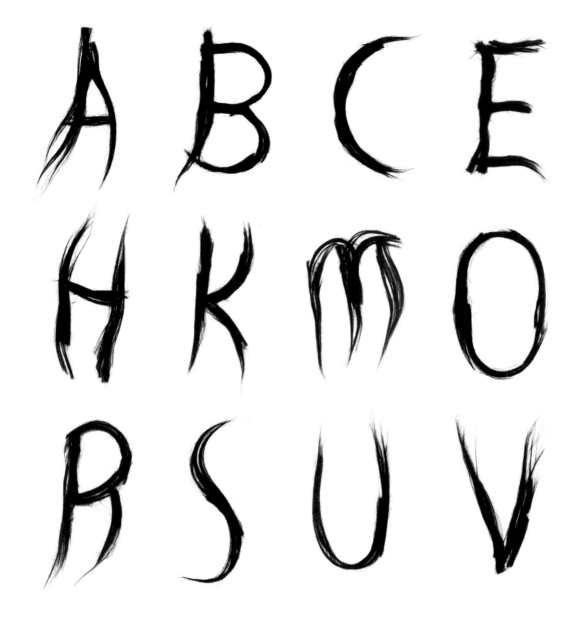

Ready-made Alphabet The challenge here
was to create a set of characters using
objects from the environment rather than
drawing them digitally or by hand. The
designers discovered letterforms hidden
in the things around them. Experimental
Typography. Nolen Strals and Bruce
Willen, faculty.

Jennifer Baghieri

Oliver Munday

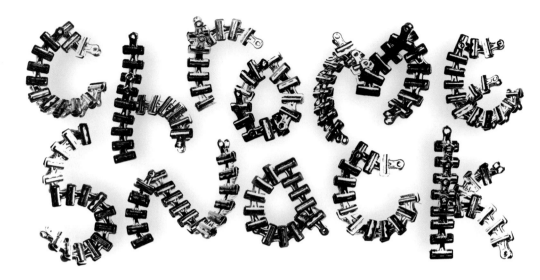

Kirby Matherne

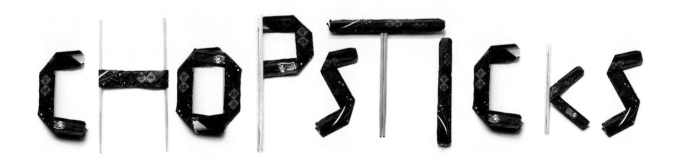

Kirsten Young

FOLD Q

K ♦ J ♣

A ♠ Q ♥

Rob McConnell

KOSHER PASTA AND MEAT SAUCE

DEF

JKL

Rotini Type Modular type can be made from anything: from digital circles and squares, scraps of paper, even bits of pasta assembled by the dozens into familiar letter shapes. Alex Jacque, Lettering & Type. Bruce Willen and Nolen Strals, faculty.

Manual Type In this project, designers use everyday objects, such as candy, nails, and hair pins, as modular units to build a word or phrase. Group cooperation yields large-scale results. Sarah Clement, Beth Cole, Kaveh Haerian, Jessica Pavone, Qianfei Wang (top); Teresa Bonaddio, Nikki Eastman, Chelsea Maymon, Storm Sebastian, Rachel Ventura (bottom), Post-Baccalaureate Studio. Jason Gottlieb, Ann Liu Alcasabas, and Sandra Maxa, faculty.

Sheena Crawley, Nick Emrich, Shuyi Meng, Kelly Nealon, Tiffany Small

Becca Friedman, Daniel Khang, Bonnie Silverberg, Mina Radojevic, Meena Yi

Min Bae, Shiraz Gallab, Anne Marie Jasinowski, Hadley Robin, Alejandro Salinas

THE QUICK BROWN FOX JUMPS OVER THE LAZY DOG

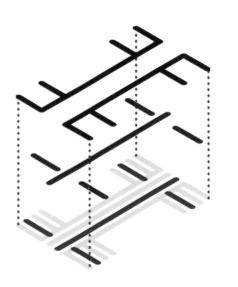 

Type as Tool This type family, called Teip, is designed with several styles and weights that users can remix into endless combinations. Elements appear to pass over and behind each other, creating a feeling of depth. Uppercase letters are stressed vertically, while lowercase letters are stressed horizontally. Alex Jacque, Graduate Type Design. Tal Leming, faculty.

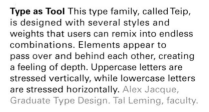  

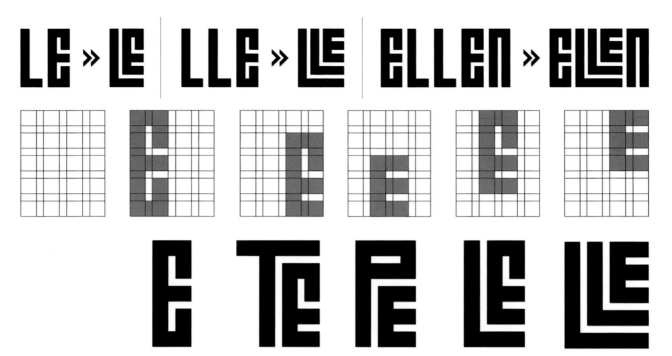

Interlocking Forms Called Barin, this typeface was inspired by the geometric kufi calligraphy prevalent in Islamic culture, especially by the work of Persian calligraphers Hassan Massoudy and Emin. A calligrapher can freely adjust a character in relation to the marks coming before and after. In contrast, a typeface designer makes each glyph function with any other glyph in any order, compromising freedom in exchange for standardization. Barin explores the line between lettering and type design. Several alternates for every glyph allow letters to interlock. Barin has more than 5,800 glyphs. Open Type features created by Tal Leming enable Barin to automatically choose among thousands of ligatures based on context. This allows the typeface to interlock and maintain the balance between negative and positive space. Shiva Nallaperumal, Graduate Type Design. Tal Leming, faculty.

Symbol Systems

A symbol stands for or represents objects, functions, and processes. Many familiar symbols, such as McDonald's golden arches, are highly distilled, stripped of extraneous detail, delivering just enough information to convey meaning. Symbol systems are often based on geometric modules that come together to create myriad forms and functions.

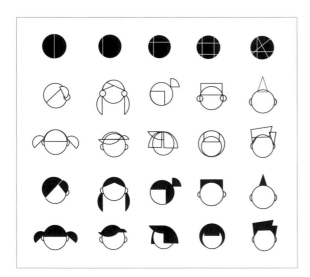

Modular Hairdos Geometrically derived forms combine to shape myriad hair styles. Yue Tuo, MFA Studio.

Counterform Pictures Counters extracted from letters in a title cohere into visual narratives. Nolen Strals and Bruce Willen, Post Typography.

Symbolscape This landscape is built and
described by a series of modularly structured
symbols stacked and layered to denote
fauna, flora, and form. Yue Tuo, MFA Studio.

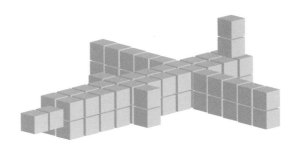

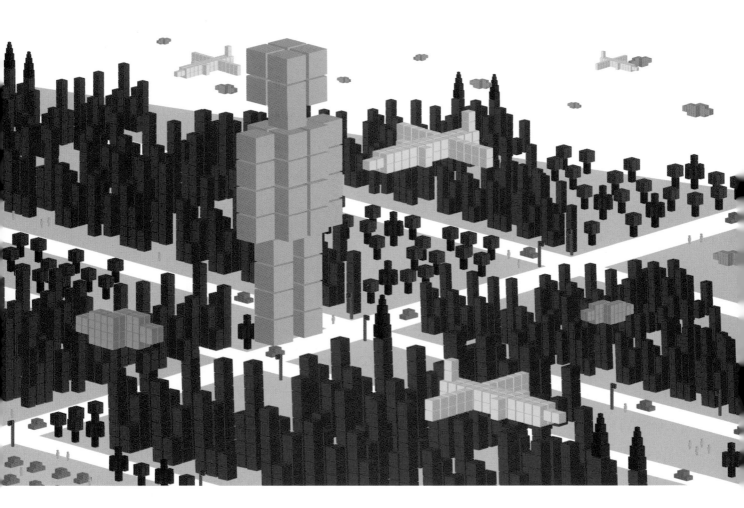

A City of Cubes An urban landscape teems with people, planes, clouds, automobiles, skyscrapers, and trees—all built from cubes in Adobe Illustrator. Yong Seuk Lee, MFA Studio.

Extrapolations in Excel These elaborate
drawings utilize the gridded compartments
of an Excel spreadsheet as a catalyst and a
constraint. Danielle Aubert, MFA thesis, Yale
University School of Art.

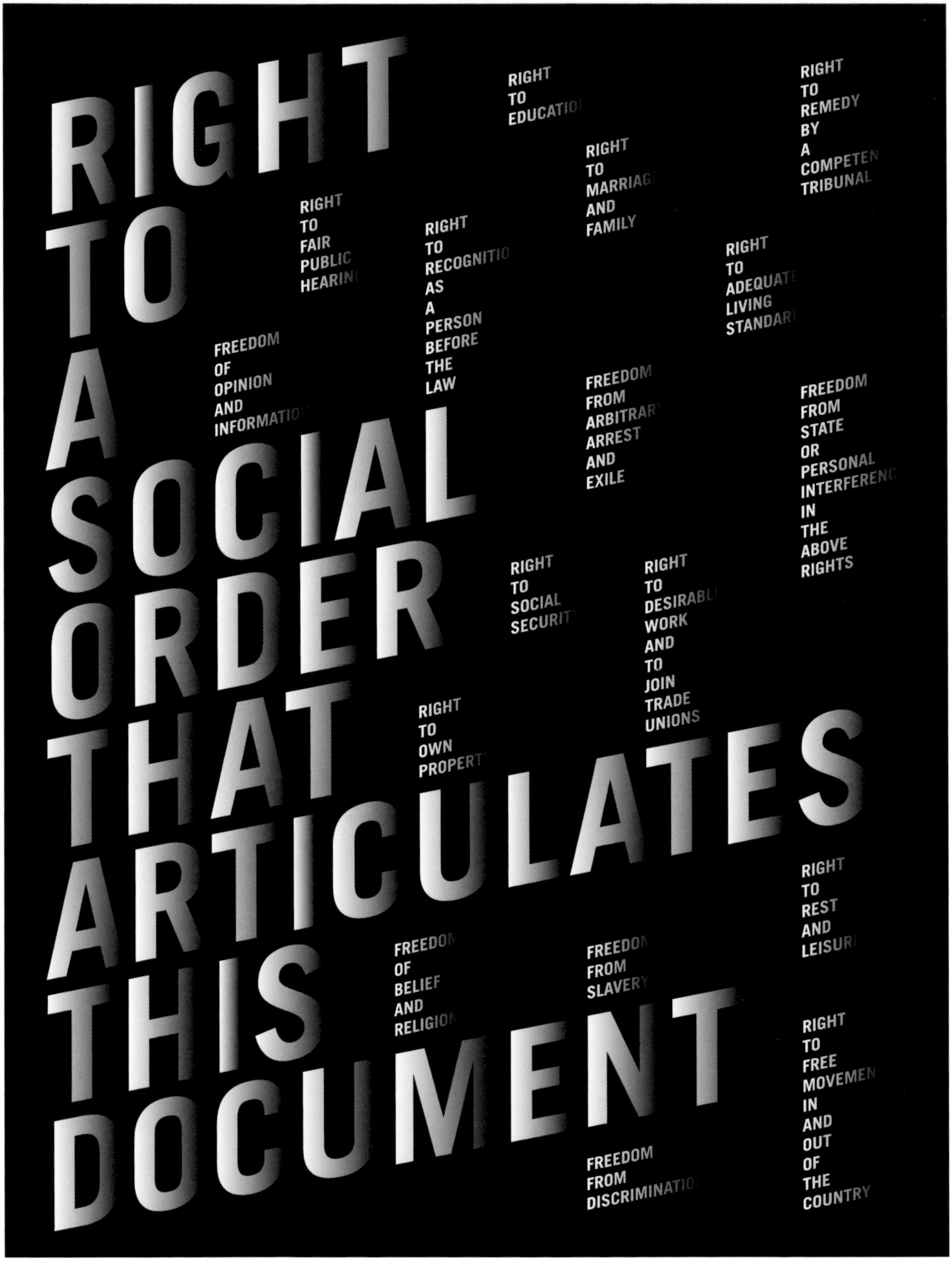

RIGHT TO A SOCIAL ORDER THAT ARTICULATES THIS DOCUMENT

RIGHT TO EDUCATION

RIGHT TO MARRIAGE AND FAMILY

RIGHT TO REMEDY BY A COMPETENT TRIBUNAL

RIGHT TO FAIR PUBLIC HEARING

RIGHT TO RECOGNITION AS A PERSON BEFORE THE LAW

RIGHT TO ADEQUATE LIVING STANDARD

FREEDOM OF OPINION AND INFORMATION

FREEDOM FROM ARBITRARY ARREST AND EXILE

FREEDOM FROM STATE OR PERSONAL INTERFERENCE IN THE ABOVE RIGHTS

RIGHT TO SOCIAL SECURITY

RIGHT TO DESIRABLE WORK AND TO JOIN TRADE UNIONS

RIGHT TO OWN PROPERTY

RIGHT TO REST AND LEISURE

FREEDOM OF BELIEF AND RELIGION

FREEDOM FROM SLAVERY

RIGHT TO FREE MOVEMENT IN AND OUT OF THE COUNTRY

FREEDOM FROM DISCRIMINATION

Grid

Typography is mostly an act of **dividing** a limited surface. Willi Baumeister

A grid is a network of lines. The lines in a grid typically run horizontally and vertically in evenly spaced increments, but grids can be angled, irregular, or even circular as well.

When you write notes on a pad of lined paper, or sketch out a floor plan on graph paper, or practice handwriting or calligraphy on ruled pages, the lines serve to guide the hand and eye as you work.

Grids function similarly in the design of printed matter. Guidelines help the designer align elements in relation to each other. Consistent margins and columns create an underlying structure that unifies the pages of a document and makes the layout process more efficient. In addition to organizing the active content of the page (text and images), the grid lends structure to the white spaces, which cease to be merely blank and passive voids but participate in the rhythm of the overall system.

A well-made grid encourages the designer to vary the scale and placement of elements without relying wholly on arbitrary or whimsical judgments. The grid offers a rationale and a starting point for each composition, converting a blank area into a structured field.

Many artists have embraced the grid as a rational, universal form that exists outside of the individual producer. At the same time, the grid is culturally associated with modern urbanism, architecture, and technology. The facades of many glass high rises and other modern buildings consist of uniform ribbons of metal and glass that wrap the building's volume in a continuous skin. In contrast with the symmetrical hierarchy of a classical building, with its strong entranceway and tiered pattern of windows, a gridded facade expresses a democracy of elements.

Grids function throughout society. The street grids used in many modern cities around the globe promote circulation among neighborhoods and the flow of traffic, in contrast with the suburban cul-de-sac, a dead-end road that keeps neighborhoods closed off and private.

The grid imparts a similarly democratic character to page and screen. By marking space into numerous equal units, the grid makes the entire surface available for use; the edges become as important as the center. Grids help designers create active, asymmetrical compositions in place of static, centered ones. By breaking down space into units, grids encourage designers to leave some areas open rather than filling up the whole page.

Software interfaces encourage the use of grids by making it easy to establish margins, columns, and page templates. Guidelines can be quickly dragged, dropped, and deleted and made visible or invisible at will. (Indeed, it is a good idea when working on screen to switch off the guidelines from time to time, as they can create a false sense of fullness and structure as well as clutter one's view.)

This chapter looks at the grid as a means of generating form, arranging images, and organizing information. The grid can work quietly in the background, or it can assert itself as an active element. The grid becomes visible as objects come into alignment with it. Some designers use grids in a strict, absolute way, while others see them as a starting point in an evolving process. This book is designed with a strong grid, but when an image or layout needs to break step with the regiment, it is allowed to do so.

Social Order The designer has used a strict grid to organize the content, while employing a gradient tone and skewed geometry to give the piece motion. Chen Yu, Typography II.

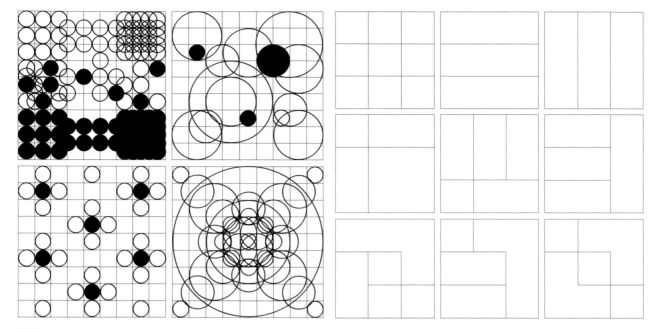

Grids Generate Form The cells and nodes of a grid can be used to generate complex pattern designs as well as simple rectangles. Dividing a square into nine identical units is a classic design problem. Numerous simple forms and relationships can be built against this simple matrix. Jason Okutake and John P. Corrigan, MFA Studio.

Form and Content

The grid has a long history within modern art and design as a means for generating form. You can construct compositions, layouts, and patterns by dividing a space into fields and filling in or delineating its cells in different ways. Try building irregular and asymmetric compositions against the neutral, ready-made backdrop of a grid. The same formal principles apply to organizing text and images in a publication design.

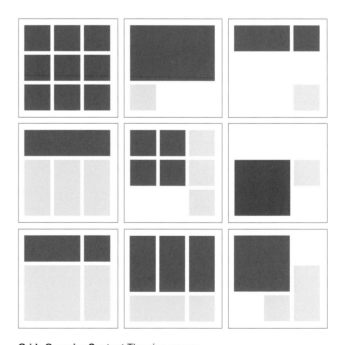

Grids Organize Content The nine-square grid divides the page into spaces for images and text. Although each layout has its own rhythm and scale, the pages are unified by the grid's underlying structure. The book you are reading is built around a similar nine-square grid. John P. Corrigan, MFA Studio.

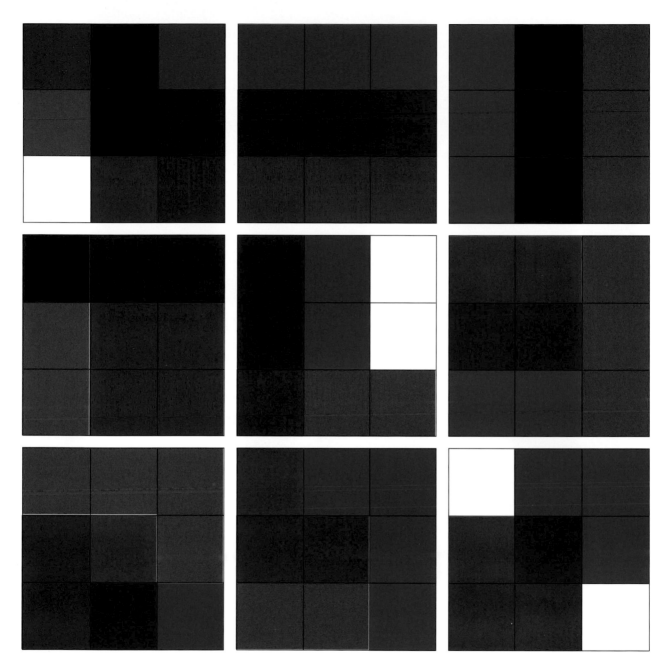

Nine-square Grid: Color Fields The grid
provides a structure for organizing fields
of color that frame and overlap each other.
Complexity emerges against a simple
armature. John P. Corrigan, MFA Studio.

Breakbeat.is & Nerve Productions
kynna í samstarfi við Heineken:

☆ Heineken

Frá DK

Pyro

Nerve   Industry   Outbreak
Leet   Habit

Á næturklúbbnum Kapital   DJ Bjöggi Nightshock
Fimmtudaginn 5. febrúar kl. 21-01   breakbeat.is
500 kr. inn | 18 ár | Skilríki skilyrði

                              DJ Lelli
                              breakbeat.is

                              DJ Tryggvi
                              breakbeat.is

Ragnar Freyr

Breakbeat.is,
Heineken & Dátinn kynna:

Breakbeat.is
á Akureyri

Kalli   **Ewok**   **Lelli**

Á skemmtistaðnum   Föstudaginn 15. júlí   Aðgangur ókeypis
Dátanum   kl. 00:00 – 04:00   20 ára aldurstakmark

✦ Heineken

Árslistakvöld
Breakbeat.is

Klute

Breakbeat.is ásamt Heineken kynna:

Commercial Suicide   Leikhúskjallaranum   20 ára aldurstakmark
Metalheadz   Laugardaginn 22. janúar   Skilríki skilyrði
Hospital   kl. 23:00   Miðaverð kr. 1000

Kalli   **Lelli**   **Gunni Ewok**

★ Heineken

Breakbeat.is
í samstarfi við
Tuborg kynnir:

Útgáfupartý
veggspjaldabókarinnar
Taktabrot

UK | R&S | Hessle Audio

Blawan

IS

Breakbeat.is DJ's

Faktorý
Smiðjustíg 6
22.00–04.30

24.03.2012
Laugardagskvöld

TUBORG

Rhythm, Form, Frame Iceland-based
designer Ragnar Freyr creates posters,
identities, websites, and publications. In
the posters shown here, Freyr has used
the grid to establish simple rhythms and
hierarchies as well as to frame images and
generate complex forms. Design: Ragnar
Freyr. Photography (left): Kevin McAuley.
Photography (below): Cleveland Aaron/
Knowledge Mag.

Breakbeat.is
& Heineken kynna:

Heineken

Árslisti
breakbeat.is
2003

Fram koma

Dj Lelli	Dj Kalli	Dj Gunni
Dj Elli	Dj Björn Ingi	Dj Guise
Dj Bjöggi	Dj Maggi	Dj Impulse
Dj Tryggvi	Dj Óli ofur	Dj Bjarki Sveins

Fastanúðar breakbeat.is fara yfir
öll bestu drum & bass lög síðasta
árs ásamt góðum gestum.

Árslistinn verður einnig kynntur
samdægurs í breakbeat.is
þættinum á X-inu 97.7

Föstudaginn 23. janúar kl. 22:00
Næturklúbburinn Kapital
20 ára inn | Skilríki skilyrði

Nánari upplýsingar á
www.breakbeat.is

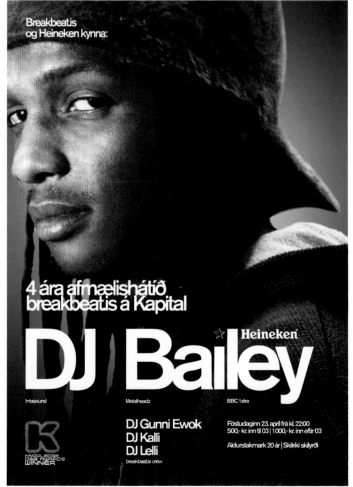

Breakbeatis
og Heineken kynna:

4 ára afmælishátíð
breakbeatis á Kapital

DJ Bailey
Heineken

Intasound

Metalheadz

BBC 1xtra

DJ Gunni Ewok
DJ Kalli
DJ Lelli

breakbeatis crew

Föstudaginn 23. apríl frá kl. 22:00
500,- kr. inn til 03 | 1000,- kr. inn eftir 03

Aldurstakmark 20 ár | Skilríki skilyrði

KNOWLEDGE D&B AWARDS
WINNER

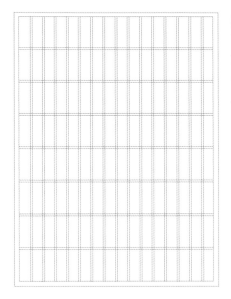

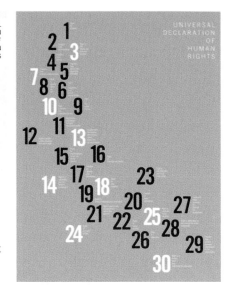

Structure and Color In this project, designers explore the grid as a tool for organizing content and generating form. The text is the United Nations' Universal Declaration of Human Rights (abbreviated version). With sixteen vertical columns and eight horizontal rows, the grid provides a flexible scaffold for organizing content. Typefaces are limited to the Univers family. After designers arrive at a solid black-and-white concept, they use color to emphasize or counteract the underlying structure.

Typography II. Ellen Lupton, faculty.

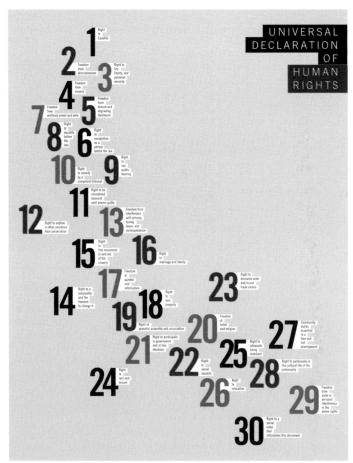

Diane Yang

Trace Byrd

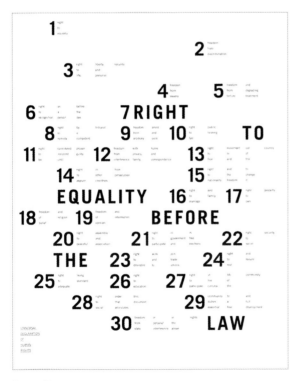

Devon Burgoyne

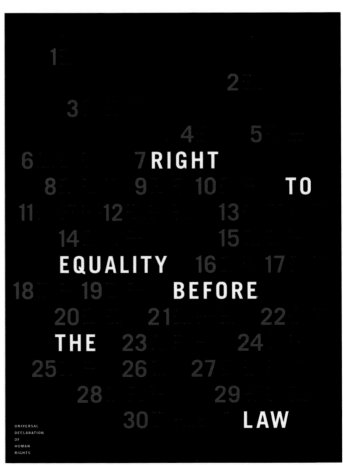

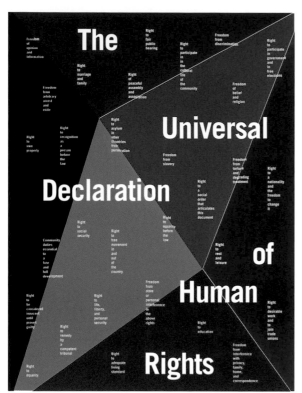

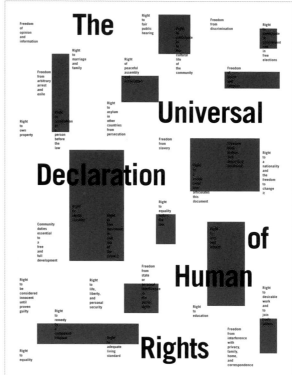

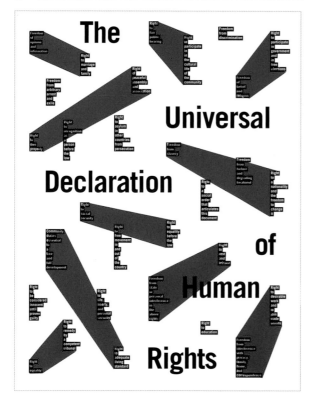

Co-Design: Generate Form After using the 16-column grid to organize the text, the designer exchanged his InDesign file with classmates and asked them to add elements based on the grid. He created the final poster at right in response to the designs he collected. Chen Yu, Typography II.

The Universal Declaration of Human Rights

Freedom of opinion and information

Right to marriage and family

Freedom from arbitrary arrest and exile

Right to fair public hearing

Right of peaceful assembly and association

Right to participate in in the cultural life of the community

Freedom from discrimination

Right to participate in government and in free elections

Freedom of belief and religion

Right to recognition as a person before the law

Right to asylum in other countries from persecution

Right to own property

Freedom from slavery

Freedom from torture and degrading treatment

Right to a social order that articulates this document

Right to a nationality and the freedom to change it

Community duties essential to a free and full development

Right to social security

Right to equality before the law

Right to rest and leisure

Right to free movement in and out of the country

Right to be considered innocent until proven guilty

Right to life, liberty, and personal security

Freedom from state or personal interference in the above rights

Right to desirable work and to join trade unions

Right to remedy by a competent tribunal

Right to adequate living standard

Right to education

Freedom from interference with privacy, family, home, and correspondence

Right to equality

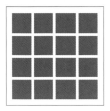

Content Management

A standard narrative book is designed with a single-column grid: one block of body copy is surrounded by margins that function as a simple frame for the content. For hundreds of years, Bibles have been designed with pages divided into two columns. Textbooks, dictionaries, reference manuals, and other books containing large amounts of text often use a two-column grid, breaking up space and making the pages less overwhelming for readers.

Magazines typically use grids with three or more vertical divisions. Multiple columns guide the placement of text, headlines, captions, images, and other page elements. One or more horizontal "hang lines" provide additional structure. A skilled designer uses a grid actively, not passively, allowing the modules to suggest intriguing shapes and surprising placements for elements.

Many Columns, Many Choices The page layouts shown here from *Print* magazine, designed by Pentagram, employ a complex, multicolumn grid. The column structure gives the pages their vertical grain, while horizontal hang lines anchor each spread, bringing elements into taut alignment. The grid helps the layout designer create active, varied pages that are held together by an underlying structure. The grid accommodates a mix of sizes and proportions in both image and text blocks. And, where appropriate, the designer breaks the grid altogether. Abbott Miller and John Kudos, Pentagram. *Print* magazine.

INTRO OUTCOME **PROCESS** EXHIBITION COLOPHON

View the App

On outcomes and intentions.

Looking backwards, I can see that my thesis project followed the classic narrative arc: **exposition, catalyst, conflict, climax, then resolution.** In other words, triumph only after a whole pile of struggle. The other sections show you the clean, polished exterior of the project; this shows you the messy insides. I love the outcome of this project, but the best thing I did this year was learn how to work through a challenge.

EXPOSITION
CATALYST
CONFLICT
CLIMAX
RESOLUTION

👆 Click below to see larger images.

White as snow is an experiment in digital narrative. This interactive book for adults mixes historical context, sociological analysis, and visual surprise with more traditional text-based storytelling to shed light on the Grimms' classic tale. Reading White as snow is an act of uncovering and creating, a new means of exercising the imagination.

Sounds like a tidy little package, right? It didn't start that way. In fact, I began the project without really knowing what it would amount to. Instead of justifying the outcome, I want to tell you about my process. My story is not unique: it is the story of a creative person trying to balance beauty and meaning.

I designed and developed White as snow in only a fraction of the amount of time that I worked on this project. Before my ideas popped out on screen, they tumbled around in my brain for what seemed like an eternity. Before I felt accomplished, I felt lost; before I had a breakthrough, I had a lot of failures.

We all grew up reading stories. If not reading, then listening; if not listening, then watching. Humans like a good narrative. Stories allow us to escape, to live other lives for a moment. They let us imagine who we might be in another world or who we might become in this one.

White as snow is the culminating work of my time in the Masters program in graphic design at Maryland Institute College of Art. I had a very personal goal for my thesis year. Rather than trying to develop a polished showpiece, I wanted to find a new way to work, expose myself to new parts of the discipline, and shake off the stagnation I felt before starting graduate school.

You would probably believe me if I said White as snow was inspired by my childhood. I could tell you about how I grew up reading fairy tales, and how by 4th grade I had read every book in my elementary school. These things are true, but they were not at the front of my mind when I embarked upon this project.

Instead of starting with content, I started with the desire to create unfiltered imagery through intuitive exploration, to think through making instead of the other way around. I saw my peers use this method to produce striking work, and I worried that my practice suffered from a certain pragmatism and predictability. With much of my career spent on corporate websites and applications, I feared that my skills were devoted far more to function than form. I wanted my work to be exciting, for myself as much as for my clients, and I decided that the thesis project would be the ideal time to step out of my comfort zone and become the designer I wanted to be.

This imagining, this placing of oneself in a story, is particularly easy with fairy tales. Records of these stories are often quite plain, forcing the audience to fill in the details. Take Snow White: she is described only as beautiful and young, with red lips, white skin, and black hair. Is she tall or short, thin or curvy? Is she smart, talkative, stubborn, athletic, kind, jealous, lazy, funny, or mean? We have to decide for ourselves.

I set up parameters that would force me to branch out. I chose narrative content to create something that tells a story rather than solving a problem. I landed on Snow White, material that's familiar enough to be recognizable but not too well known, not boring or repetitive. I mined the story for visual content, listing colors, objects, characters: anything I could find that might give birth to imagery.

And so it began, experimentation with no outcome in mind. My only goal was to make anything and everything I could and without succumbing to over-analysis. I created 100 representations of the apple. I marbleized stills from the 1938 Disney film. I created icon sets to represent important scenes, gradients to evoke these scenes, and spoof iPhone apps that a modern-day Queen could use to calculate her beauty. I painted. I drew. I took pictures. I made vector illustrations. I collaged.

Some of this work is beautiful and some conveys the story in an interesting way, but to me it all felt empty. Without knowing what I was trying to communicate and why, I had no value system on which to evaluate what I made. Yes, the point was to avoid evaluating things too soon, but I had no drive to move forward without such judgement. I quickly ran out of steam. In hopes of inspiring new ideas, I broadened my research and began to explore the context of Snow White.

The Grimm brothers did not think up their work, they simply recorded German folklore. They thought these stories represented German identity, the essence of the people. It's an odd set of values to hold dear: narcissism, cruelty, and revenge.

I was excited by what I found. And when I spoke about it, my peers and mentors were excited too. They were intrigued by the Grimm brothers, surprised by the parallels between Snow White and Jesus, and in love with the cheeky psychoanalysis that came to me much more easily than imagery.

My ideas were interesting, but they still didn't translate into good work. In one hand I had piles of visuals and in the other I had writing; I could not fit them together. I thought that designing through intuition meant that I couldn't force meaning into my work, but I couldn't find any other way to create.

I almost gave up. I cursed myself for trying to develop a new method so far from my comfort zone. Instead of just backing off a little, I fell into full-on analytical mode. I stopped painting apples and started making spreadsheets. I took a detour into design-about-design and I tried to tell the story of Snow White through the steps of user experience design. It didn't work; my meta-project flopped.

There are Snow White tales all over the world. Why is it that so many people in so many places would pass it on? Perhaps it's because of the universal nature of its ideas. Beauty and youth, female sexuality, tension between mothers and daughters: these issues run deep.

Process is personal. There is no one right way to create. On the first day of grad school, I attended a workshop led by Paul Sahre and Joe Miller. Sahre was asked...

Digital Grids The webpage at left features a single column of text edged with reference images; users can click on an image for an enlarged view. This simple structure is similar to that of many online newspapers. The pages above are examples of responsive layout; the grid changes depending on the output device. Emma Sherwood-Forbes and Nour Tabet, MFA Studio.

Automated Grids

Grids for digital media are often built on the fly to organize chunks of content into collections of data that users can quickly scan. Google searches and Pinterest boards present images in grids whose irregular heartbeat reflects the diverse shapes and sizes of content. Pinterest accommodates the long, skinny graphics made popular by vertically scrolling websites, while Google image searches favor horizontal images. The web's random sense of overflow has also inspired designers to create new grids for print.

Google Image Search: Field

Pinterest Grid

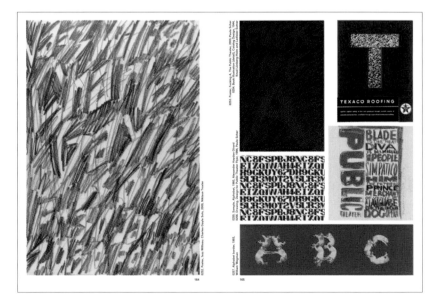

New Realities of the Page The utilitarian density of the web has influenced design for print, as seen in the book *Making Design,* published by Cooper Hewitt, Smithsonian Design Museum (2015). Irma Boom.

The End of White Space (opposite) Images lock together in a compact geometry in the pages of *Harun Farocki Diagrams,* edited and designed by Benedikt Reichenbach, Verlag der Buchhandlung Walther König (2014).

12 INEXTINGUISHABLE FIRE

13 INEXTINGUISHABLE FIRE

74 IMAGES OF THE WORLD AND THE INSCRIPTION OF WAR

75 IMAGES OF THE WORLD AND THE INSCRIPTION OF WAR

Pattern

The **principles** discoverable in the works
of the past belong to us; not so the **results**.

Owen Jones

The creative evolution of ornament spans all of human history. Shared ways to generate pattern are found in cultures around the world. Universal principles underlie diverse styles and icons that speak to particular times and traditions.

This chapter shows how to build complex patterns around core concepts. Dots, stripes, and grids provide the architecture behind an infinite range of designs. By composing a single element in different schemes, the designer can create endless variations, building complexity around a logical core.

Styles and motifs of pattern-making evolve within and among cultures, and they move in and out of fashion. They travel from place to place and time to time, carried along like viruses by the forces of commerce and the restless desire for variety.

In the twentieth century, modern designers avoided ornate detail in favor of minimal adornment. In 1908, the Viennese design critic Adolf Loos famously conflated "Ornament and Crime." He linked the human lust for decoration with primitive tattoos and criminal behavior.[1]

Yet despite the modern distaste for ornament, the structural analysis of pattern is central to modern design theory. In 1856, Owen Jones created his monumental *Grammar of Ornament*, documenting decorative vocabularies from around the world.[2] Jones's book encouraged Western designers to copy and reinterpret "exotic" motifs from Asia and Africa, but it also helped them recognize principles that unite an endless diversity of forms.

Today, surface pattern is creating a vibrant discourse. The rebirth of ornament is linked to the revival of craft in architecture, products, and interiors, as well as to scientific views of how life emerges from the interaction of simple rules.

The decorative forms presented in this chapter embrace a mix of formal structure and organic irregularity. They meld individual authorship with rule-based systems, and they merge formal abstraction with personal narrative. By understanding how to produce patterns, designers learn how to weave complexity out of elementary structures, participating in the world's most ancient and prevalent artistic practice.

Crazy Quilt Mixing and matching patterns is an ancient enterprise. Here, a mix is made with a palette of digital elements that communicate with each other. Jeremy Botts, MFA Studio.

1. Adolf Loos, *Ornament and Crime: Selected Essays* (Riverside, CA: Ariadne Press, 1998).
2. Owen Jones, *The Grammar of Ornament* (London: Day and Son, 1856).

The secret to success in all ornament is the production of a broad general effect by the repetition of **a few simple elements**.

Owen Jones

Dots, Stripes, and Grids

In the nineteenth century, designers began analyzing how patterns are made. They found that nearly any pattern arises from three basic forms: isolated elements, linear elements, and the criss-crossing or interaction of the two.[1] Various terms have been used to name these elementary conditions, but we will call them dots, stripes, and grids.

Any isolated form can be considered a dot, from a simple circle to an ornate flower. A stripe, in contrast, is a linear path. It can consist of a straight, solid line, or it can be built up from smaller elements (dots) that link together visually to form a line.

These two basic structures, dots and stripes, interact to form grids. As a grid takes shape, it subverts the identity of the separate elements in favor of a larger texture. Indeed, creating that larger texture is what pattern design is all about. Imagine a field of wildflowers. It is filled with spectacular individual organisms that contribute to an overall system.

1. Our scheme for classifying ornament is adapted from Archibald Christie, *Traditional Methods of Pattern Designing; An Introduction to the Study of the Decorative Art* (Oxford: Clarendon Press, 1910).

From Point to Line to Grid As dots move together, they form into lines and other shapes (while still being dots). As stripes cross over each other and become grids, they cut up the field into new figures, which function like new dots or new stripes.

Some of the most visually fascinating patterns result from figure/ground ambiguity. The identity of a form can oscillate between being a figure (dot, stripe) to being a ground or support for another, opposing figure.

Repeating Elements

How does a simple form—a dot, a square, a flower, a cross—populate a surface to create a pattern that calms, pleases, or surprises us?

Whether rendered by hand, machine, or code, a pattern results from repetition. An army of dots can be regulated by a rigid geometric grid, or it can randomly swarm across a surface via irregular handmade marks. It can spread out in a continuous veil or concentrate its forces in pockets of intensity.

In every instance, however, patterns follow some repetitive principle, whether dictated by a mechanical grid, a digital algorithm, or the physical rhythm of a crafts-person's tool as it works along a surface.

In the series of pattern studies developed here and on the following pages, a simple lozenge form is used to build designs of varying complexity. Experiments of this kind can be performed with countless base shapes, yielding an endless range of individual results.

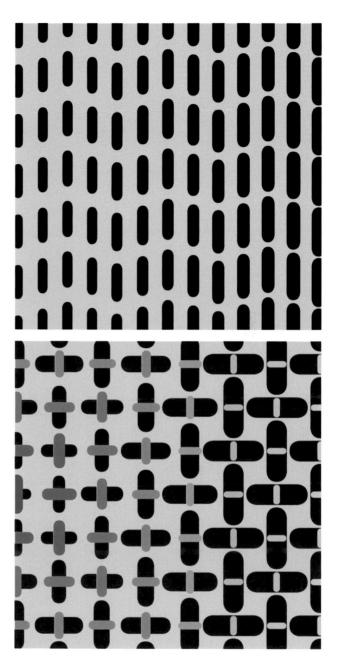

One Element, Many Patterns The basic element in these patterns is a lozenge shape. Based on the orientation, proximity, scale, and color of the lozenges, they group into overlapping lines, forming a nascent grid. Jeremy Botts, MFA Studio.

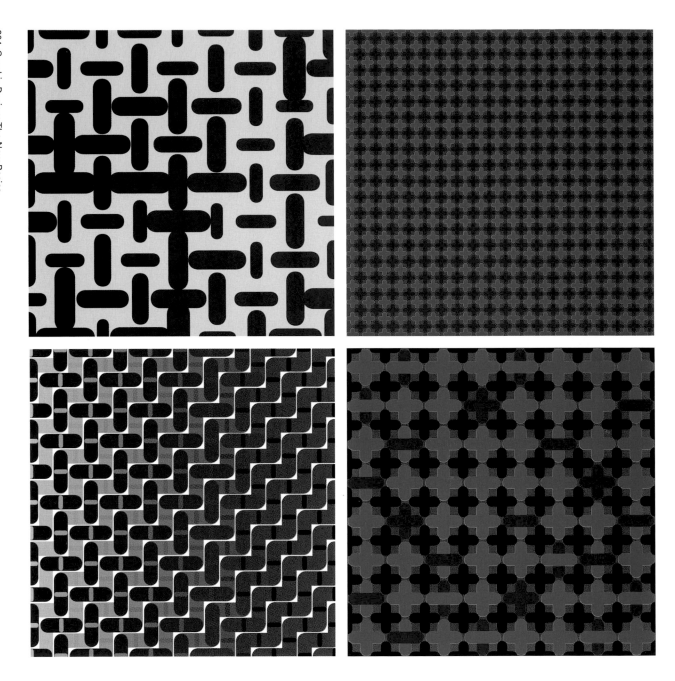

One Element, Many Patterns In this series of designs, the lozenge shape functions as a dot, the primitive element at the core of numerous variations. This oblong dot combines with other dots to form quatrefoils (a new super-dot) as well as lines.

As lozenges of common color or orientation begin to associate with each other visually, additional figures take shape across the surface. Jeremy Botts, MFA Studio.

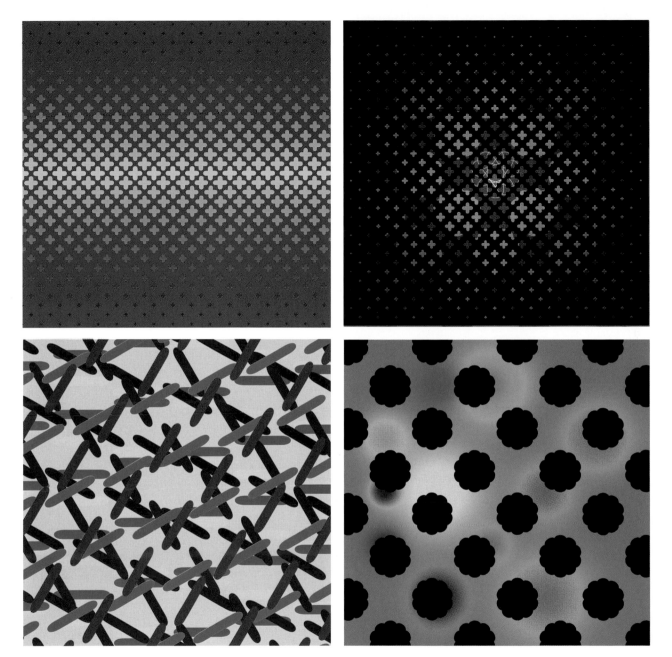

Changing Color, Scale, and Orientation
Altering the color contrast between elements or changing the overall scale of the pattern transforms its visual impact. Color shifts can be uniform across the surface, or they can take place in gradients or steps.

Turning elements on an angle or changing their scale also creates a sense of depth and motion. New figures emerge as the lozenge rotates and repeats. Jeremy Botts, MFA Studio.

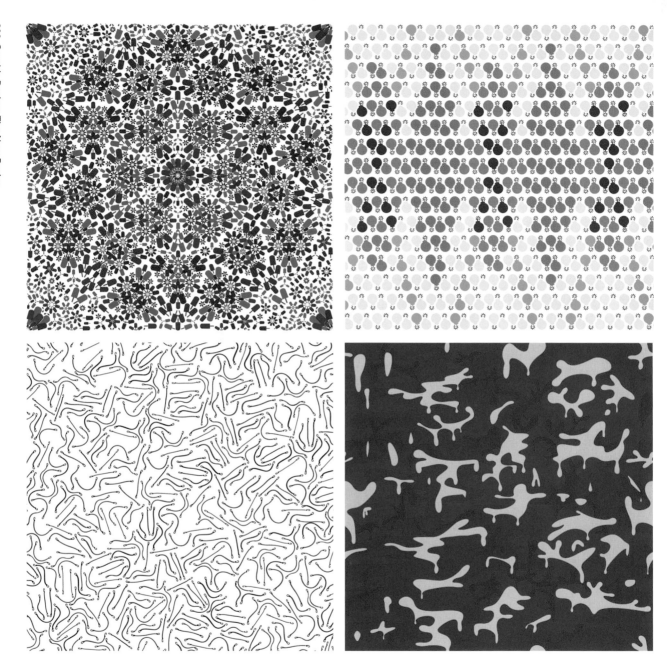

Iconic Patterns Here, traditional pattern structures have been populated with images that have personal significance for the designer: popsicles, bombs, bungee cords, yellow camouflage, and slices of bright green cake. The single tiles above can be repeated into larger patterns, as shown opposite. Spence Holman, MFA Studio.

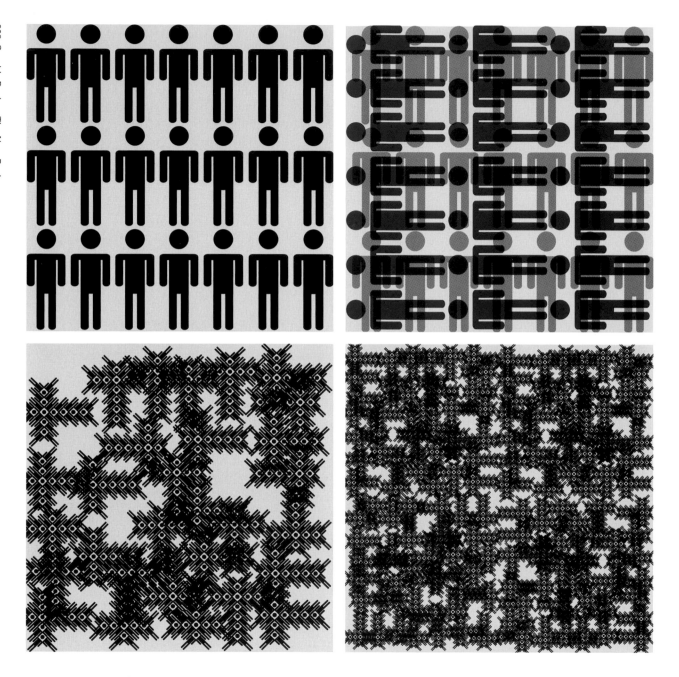

Regular and Irregular Interesting pattern designs often result from a mix of regular and irregular forces as well as abstract and recognizable imagery. Here, regimented rows of icons overlap to create dense crowds as well as orderly battalions. Yong Seuk Lee, MFA Studio.

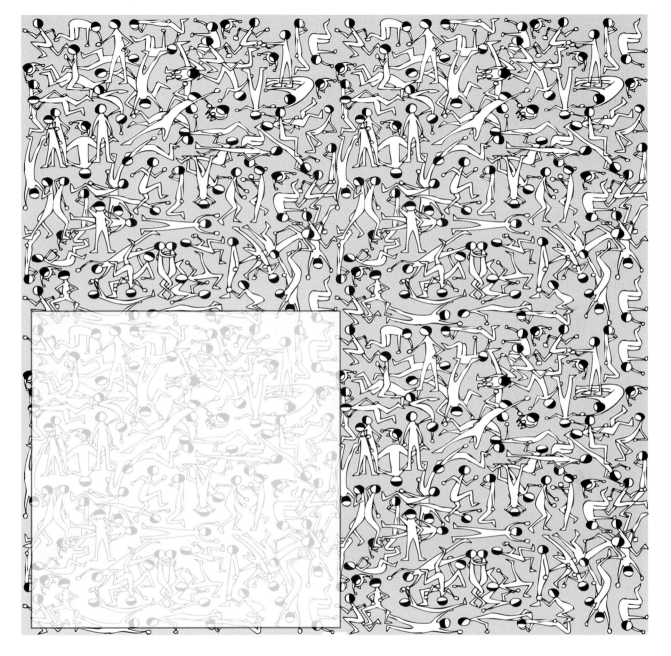

Random Repeat These patterns appear highly irregular, yet they are composed of repeating tiles. To make this kind of pattern, the designer needs to make the left and right edges and the top and bottom edges match up with those of an identical tile. Anything can take place in the middle of the tile.

The tiles shown here are square, but they could be rectangles, diamonds, or any other interlocking shape. Yong Seuk Lee, MFA Studio.

Grid as Matrix An infinite number of patterns can be created from a common grid. In the simplest patterns, each cell is turned on or off. Larger figures take shape as neighboring clusters fill in.

More complex patterns occur when the grid serves to locate forms without dictating their outlines or borders. Jason Okutake, MFA Studio.

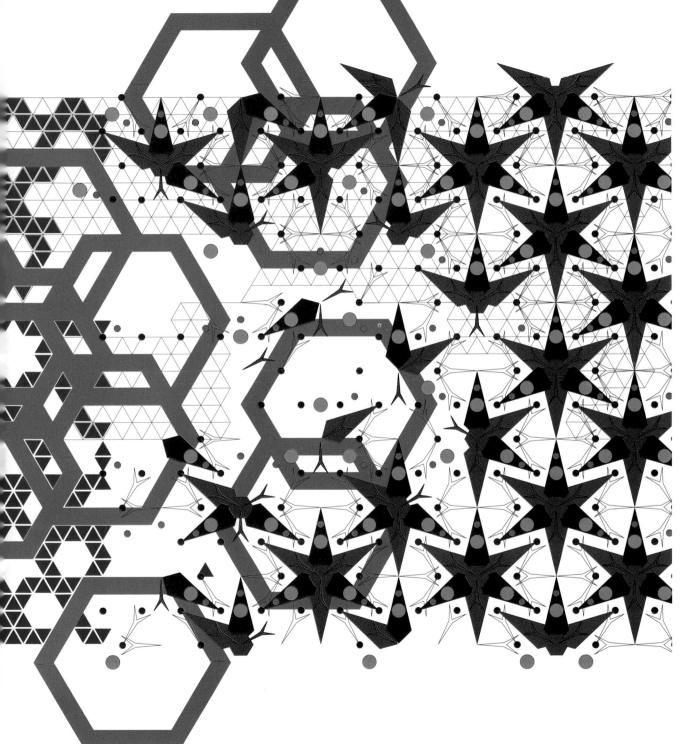

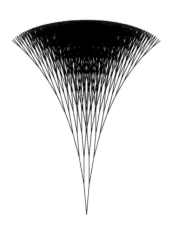

Code-Based Patterns

Every pattern follows a rule. Defining rules with computer code allows the designer to create variations by changing the input to the system. The designer creates the rule, but the end result may be unexpected.

The patterns shown here were designed using Processing, the open-source computer language created for designers and visual artists. All the patterns are built around the basic form of a binary tree, a structure in which every node yields no more than two offspring. New branches appear with each iteration of the program.

The binary tree form has been repeated, rotated, inverted, connected, and overlapped to generate a variety of pattern elements, equivalent to "tiles" in a traditional design. By varying the inputs to the code, the designer created four different tiles, which she joined together in Photoshop to produce a larger repeating pattern. The principle is no different from that used in many traditional ornamental designs, but the process has been automated, yielding a different kind of density.

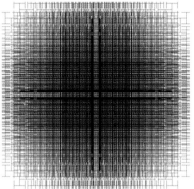

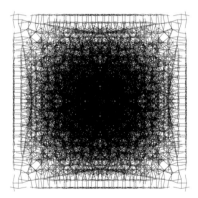

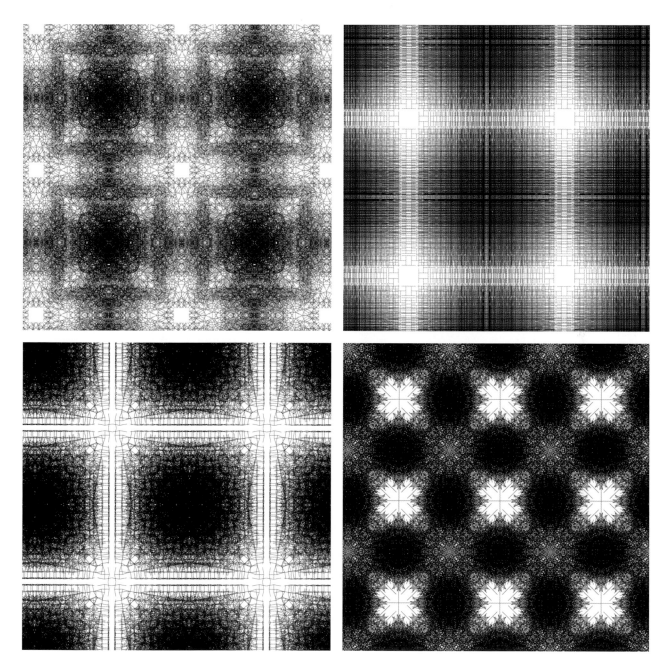

Vary the Input Four different base elements
were created by varying the input to the
code. The base "tiles" are joined together
to create a repeat pattern; new figures
emerge where the tiles come together,
just as in traditional ornament. Yeohyun Ahn,
Interactive Media II. James Ravel, faculty.

ORNAMENT · PATTERN · TYPOGRAPHY · LANGUAGE · SHINY THINGS

OBSESSIONS

WRITING

LOVE · HATE

PEOPLE*

THEMES

humour

relationships, public private communications, emotions, love, sex

words, custom type, curves, loops, curls, hooks, claws, fur, hair, pixels, drama, contrast, juxtapositions, mechanical, organic,

pencil
computer
fine pen
pen et ink
ballpoint pen
scratchboard
camera
pencil crayons
paint
paper
fabric
ribbons
beads
plants
objects

MATERIALS

*excluding those whom work I like so love, but who have no significant influence on my work

thai silks
chinese brocade
indonesian batik
indian saris et prints
ribbons et bows
embroidery
lace

TEXTILES

FASHION

COSTUME

BARCELONA

PARIS

MILAN

TORINO

KENYA

9 YEARS AS A GRAPHIC DESIGNER

renée mackintosh · antonio gaudí · hundertwasser · chris ware · naomi klein · martin woeczky · ed felix · ross mills · herman zapf · josef müller-brockman · herb lubalin · donald young · edward muybridge · ricky jay · robert bringhurst · a.a. milne

stefan sagmeister · piet zwart · victor moscoso · koloman moser · gert dunbar
brian morgan · paula scher · will bradley · el lissitzky · edward tufte · rudolf koch · alphonse mucha · moholy nagy
rick valicenti

the boere; tironwork, ingrada femina e gaudí
milan duomo et notre dame (gothic cathedral); the boere; tironwork,
thai complex; egyptian mosques; kangan carving; torino cemmetery; italian tiles; milan duomo et notre dame
temples, havelis, palaces; tile, inlaid marble et mirror; indonesian complex, balinese hinduism; thai complex; egyptian mosques;

william morris · gustav klimt · ingres · caravaggio · jenny holzer · alexander calder
arthur rackham · fred tomaselli · ed ruscha · matthew barney

inuzii
birds (feathers)
sea life
plants

insects
NATURE

ARCHITECTURE

PHOTOGRAPHY

GRAFFITI

PERSIAN CARPETS

JEWELLERY

MONEY

MAPS

STAMPS

NEW YORK CONTEMPORARY ART GALLERIES

WOOD CARVING

ENGRAVING

10 YEARS AS A BOOK TYPESETTER

CAIRO

BANGKOK

BALI

JAVA

FORMS & MOVEMENTS

mediaeval manuscripts
islamic art
baroque, rococo
victoriana
arts et crafts
art nouveau
modernism
swiss typography
psychedelia
calligraphy
dimensional typography

MISC
INFLUENCES

JERUSALEM

INDIA

TRAVEL

POLITICS

DRAWING & PAINTING

alphonse mucha poster

leonardo da vinci knotwork

flowered wallpaper pattern

THREE VERY EARLY
INFLUENCES FROM AGE
EIGHT (APPROX).

Diagram

In emphasizing evidential quality and beauty, I also want to move the practices of **analytical design** far away from the practices of propaganda, marketing, graphic design, and commercial art.

Edward R. Tufte

A diagram is a graphic representation of a structure, situation, or process. Diagrams can depict the anatomy of a creature, the hierarchy of a corporation, or the flow of ideas. Diagrams allow us to see relationships that would not come forward in a straight list of numbers or a verbal description.

Many of the visual elements and phenomena described in this book—from point, line, and plane to scale, color, hierarchy, layers, and more—converge in the design of diagrams. In the realm of information graphics, the aesthetic role of these elements remains important, but something else occurs as well. Graphic marks and visual relationships take on specific meanings, coded within the diagram to depict numerical increments, relative size, temporal change, structural links, and other conditions.

The great theorist of information design is Edward R. Tufte, who has been publishing books on this subject since 1983. Tufte finds a certain kind of beauty in the visual display of data—a universal beauty grounded in the laws of nature and the mind's ability to comprehend them.[1]

Tufte has called for removing the practice of information design from the distorting grasp of propaganda and graphic design. He argues that a chart or diagram should employ no metaphoric distractions or excessive flourishes (what he has called "chart junk"), but should stay within the realm of objective observation.

Tufte's purist point of view is profound and compelling, but it may be overly restrictive. Information graphics do have a role to play in the realm of expressive and editorial graphics. The language of diagrams has yielded a rich and evocative repertoire within contemporary design. In editorial contexts, diagrams often function to illuminate and explain complex ideas. They can be clean and reductive or richly expressive, creating evocative pictures that reveal surprising relationships and impress the eye with the sublime density and grandeur of a body of data.

Many of the examples developed in this chapter are rigorous but not pure. Some pieces use diagrams to depict personal histories, a process that forces the designer to develop systematic ways to represent subjective experience. Such an approach is seen in the extravagant autobiographical diagram presented on the page opposite, by Marian Bantjes. Her map does not aim to convey evidence in a strictly scientific way, but rather uses analytical thinking to unleash a language that is both personal and universal, building complexity around basic structures.

Map of Influences This alluring diagram by designer and artist Marian Bantjes describes her visual influences, which range from medieval and Celtic lettering, to baroque and rococo ornament, to Swiss typography and American psychedelia. Those diverse influences come alive in the flowing, filigreed lines of the piece. Marian Bantjes.

1. Edward R. Tufte, *Beautiful Evidence* (Cheshire, CT: Graphics Press, 2006).

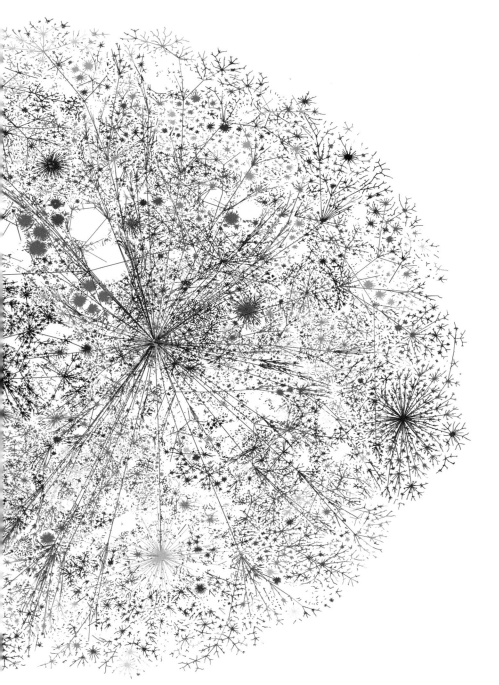

Making Connections

A network, also called a graph, is a set of connections among nodes or points.[1] There are various ways to connect the nodes in a network, resulting in different kinds of organization. Centralized networks include pyramids and trees, where all power issues from a common point. A decentralized network has a spine with radiating elements, as in an interstate highway system. A distributed network has node-to-node relationships with no spine and no center. The Internet is a distributed network peppered with concentrated nodes of connectivity.

Networks are everywhere—not just in technology, but throughout nature and society. A food chain, a city plan, and the pathway of a disease are all networks that can be described graphically with points and lines.

Decentralized Network This snapshot of the World Wide Web (detail) shows the connections among servers. A relatively small number of hubs dominate global traffic. Courtesy Lumeta Corp. © 2005 Lumeta Corp.

1. On network theory, see Alexander Galloway and Eugene Thacker, "Protocol, Control and Networks," *Grey Room* 12 (Fall 2004): 6–29. See also Christopher Alexander, "The City is Not a Tree," in Joan Ockman, ed., *Architecture Culture, 1943–1968: A Documentary Anthology* (New York: Rizzoli, 1993), 379–88.

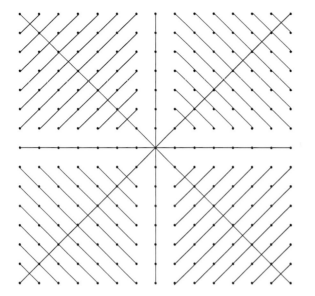

Centralized Kelly Horigan

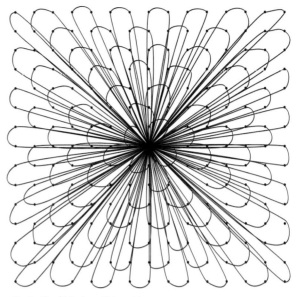

Centralized Lindsay Orlowski

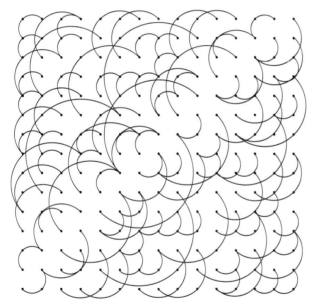

Decentralized Lindsay Orlowski

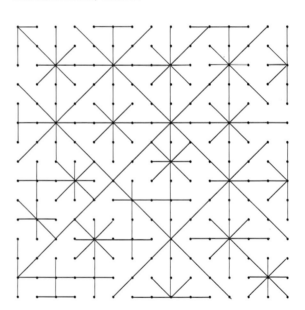

Distributed Kelly Horigan

Designing Networks In this project, designers connect a grid of dots with lines, producing designs that reflect different types of networks: centralized, decentralized, and distributed. Graphic Design II. Ellen Lupton, faculty.

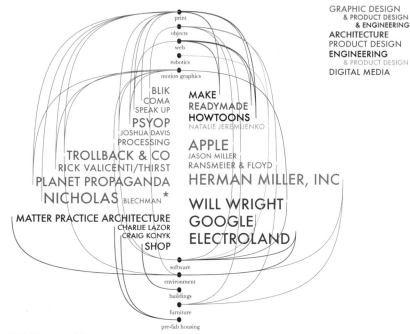

GRAPHIC DESIGN
& PRODUCT DESIGN
& ENGINEERING
ARCHITECTURE
PRODUCT DESIGN
ENGINEERING
& PRODUCT DESIGN
DIGITAL MEDIA

print
objects
web
robotics
motion graphics

BLIK
COMA
SPEAK UP
PSYOP
JOSHUA DAVIS
PROCESSING
TROLLBACK & CO
RICK VALICENTI/THIRST
PLANET PROPAGANDA
NICHOLAS BLECHMAN *
MATTER PRACTICE ARCHITECTURE
CHARLIE LAZOR
CRAIG KONYK
SHOP

MAKE
READYMADE
HOWTOONS
NATALIE JEREMIJENKO
APPLE
JASON MILLER
RANSMEIER & FLOYD
HERMAN MILLER, INC
WILL WRIGHT
GOOGLE
ELECTROLAND

software
environment
buildings
furniture
pre-fab housing

C DESIGN Alexandra Matzner

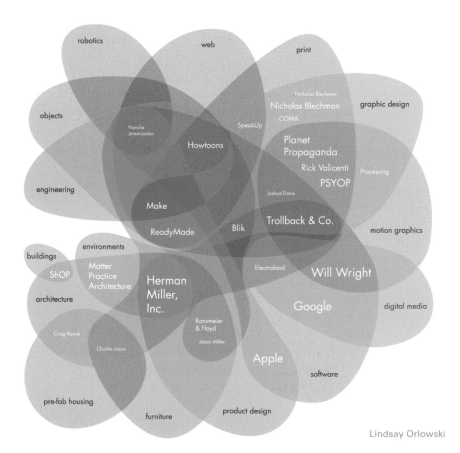

Lindsay Orlowski

Overlapping Relationships People don't fall into tidy categories. Any individual can have many identities: parent, child, professional, fan, taxpayer, and so on.

In the project shown here, students were given a list of designers and design firms who work in different fields (graphic design, architecture, and new media) and who produce different kinds of projects (buildings, websites, products, print, and so on). The list also ranked people according to the size of their firms (from single practitioners to large corporations). The design challenge was to represent these overlapping categories visually, using typography, scale, color, line, and other cues to indicate connections and differences.

Some of the solutions use dots of varying size to indicate scale or to mark points on a conceptual map. Others change the size of the typography to indicate the scale. Overlapping planes or crossing lines were used to indicate areas of overlap. This problem can be applied to any collection of objects, from a grocery list to categories of music or art. Graphic Design II. Ellen Lupton, faculty.

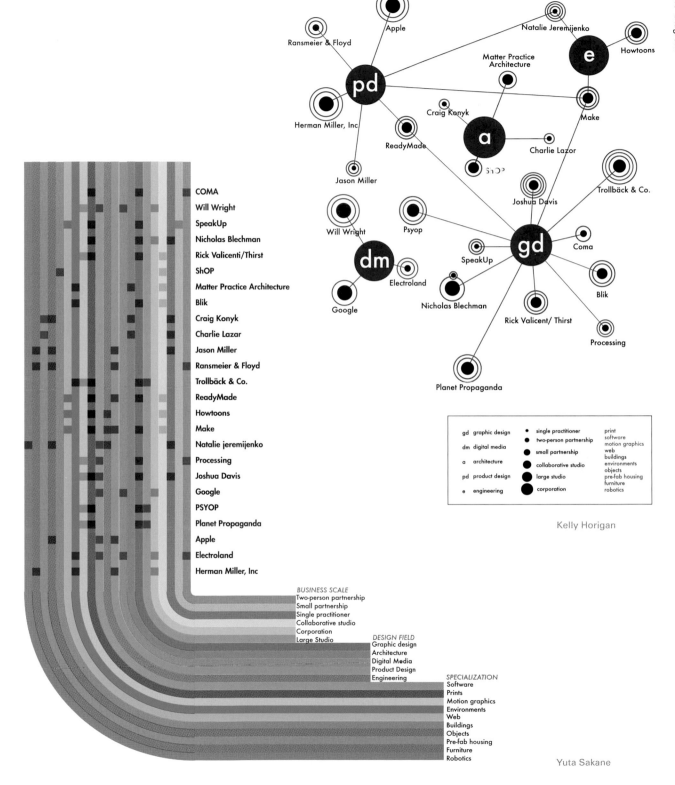

Kelly Horigan

Yuta Sakane

COMA
Will Wright
SpeakUp
Nicholas Blechman
Rick Valicenti/Thirst
ShOP
Matter Practice Architecture
Blik
Craig Konyk
Charlie Lazar
Jason Miller
Ransmeier & Floyd
Trollbäck & Co.
ReadyMade
Howtoons
Make
Natalie jeremijenko
Processing
Joshua Davis
Google
PSYOP
Planet Propaganda
Apple
Electroland
Herman Miller, Inc

BUSINESS SCALE
Two-person partnership
Small partnership
Single practitioner
Collaborative studio
Corporation
Large Studio

DESIGN FIELD
Graphic design
Architecture
Digital Media
Product Design
Engineering

SPECIALIZATION
Software
Prints
Motion graphics
Environments
Web
Buildings
Objects
Pre-fab housing
Furniture
Robotics

gd graphic design
dm digital media
a   architecture
pd product design
e   engineering

• single practitioner
• two-person partnership
● small partnership
● collaborative studio
● large studio
● corporation

print
software
motion graphics
web
buildings
environments
objects
pre-fab housing
furniture
robotics

63THINGSABOUTDESIGN

05 FAVOURITETYPEFACES

Akzidenz-Grotesk	Bodoni	EasyScript	Fedra Mono	BaseMono	Interstate
1986	1813	2008	2002	1997	1999
a c e	a c e	a c e	a c e	a c e	a c e
b d f	b d f	b d f	b d f	b d f	b d f
g i k	g i k	g i k	g i k	g i k	g i k
h j l	h j l	h j l	h j l	h j l	h j l
m o q	m o q	m o q	m o q	m o q	m o q
n p r	n p r	n p r	n p r	n p r	n p r
s u w	s u w	s u w	s u w	s u w	s u w
t v x	t v x	t v x	t v x	t v x	t v x
y z	y z	y z	y z	y z	y z

06 COLOURHARMONIES

Complementary	(A+G)
Analogous	(H+G+F)
Split-Complementary	(K+I+D)
Triadic	(J+B+F)
Tetradic	(B+H+L+F)
Square	(A+G+D+J)

05 GOODBOOKSABOUTTYPOGRAPHY

01	1967 **Typographie: A Manual of Design** EMIL RUDER
02	2004 **The Elements of Typographic Style** ROBERT BRINGHURST
03	2011 **A Type Primer** JOHN KANE
04	1928 **Die Neue Typographie** JAN TSISCHOLD
05	1961 **Grid Systems in Graphic Design** JOSEF MÜLLER-BROCKMANN

02 PAPERANDWASTEINTHEUSA

PAPER ACCOUNTS FOR MORE THAN A THIRD OF ALL RECYCLABLES COLLECTED IN THE US, BY WEIGHT.

IN 2010, THE AMOUNT OF PAPER RECOVERED FOR RECYCLING AVERAGED 334 POUNDS FOR EACH PERSON LIVING IN THE U.S.

Big Content This ambitious project challenges designers to organize a diverse array of content (text and diagrams) within a long, compressed banner. Designers explore principles of grid, hierarchy, color, and flow in order to create effective layouts. Left to right: Nicolas Kubail Kalousdian, Bonnie Silverman, Shiraz Gallab, Typography II. Ellen Lupton, faculty.

12 PRODUCTSMADEUSINGRECYCLEDPAPER

06 LAWSOFVISUALGROUPING

Continuity

Simplicity

Closure

Left Page

75 THINGS YOU NEED TO KNOW ABOUT GRAPHIC DESIGN

BY BONNIE SILVERBERG

GRAPHIC DESIGN IS *A tool that's used everywhere. It changes people's minds while making the world prettier. Think of it this way, it is the polish but not the shoe.*

6 TYPE CRIMES
TOP OFFENDERS

Ugly rag (*inexcusable*). River (*gasp*). Two word spaces between sentences. Pseudo italics (*awful*). Dumb quotes. Pseudo small caps (*please stop now*).

STILL NOT GETTING IT? MUST I SHOW EXAMPLES? FINE.

This block of text has an **UGLY RAG.** The space after the text on each line is appalling. Not to mention the **DOUBLE WORD SPACE** after each sentence.

Not everything can be as beautifully aligned as this document. Faking it can create vertical and horizontal gaps (**RIVERS**) that are very distracting.

I asked to be quoted. Not to have vertical lines (**DUMB QUOTES**) added to my copy". Shall we try it again? "Perfect". Now this is how to properly quote a quote."

Is it cue? Or is this sentence on a slant? This is **ITALIC.** Finally, here is a **SMALL CAP** (*cute*). They are not the same as CAPITAL LETTERS SHRUNKEN DOWN. Don't do it. It's a type crime!

6 LAWS OF VISUAL GROUPING

CLOSURE · SYMMETRY · CONTINUITY · SIMILARITY · PROXIMITY · SIMPLICITY

3 TYPES OF DASHES

EN DASH (–): for dates and time. **EM DASH** (—): summarizes a thought. **HYPHEN** (-): joins words together.

[5 FAVORITE TYPEFACES]

TUNGSTEN: SMART, TOUGH & SEXY
MR. EAVES: SMALL X-HEIGHT
GOTHAM: BIG, CLEAN & EASY
DIDOT: ALWAYS FASHIONABLE
ARCHER: SLAB SERIF DONE RIGHT

334 The amount of pounds of paper recovered for recycling for each person in the U.S. Paper accounts for more than a third of all recyclables collected in the U.S. by weight. Blue paper recycle bins work.

5 GOOD BOOKS ABOUT TYPOGRAPHY

Emil Ruder, **TYPOGRAPHIE: A MANUAL OF DESIGN**, 1967 (*top notch*)
Robert Bringhurst, **THE ELEMENTS OF TYPOGRAPHIC STYLE**, 2004
John Kane, **A TYPE PRIMER**, 2011 (*hard to miss the bright cover*)
Simon Garfield, **JUST MY TYPE**, 2012 (*typography humor for all*)
Steven Heller, **100 IDEAS THAT CHANGED GRAPHIC DESIGN**, 2012

8 PRODUCTS MADE FROM RECYCLED PAPER

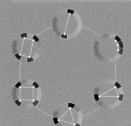

GLOBES · DUST MASKS · MASKING TAPE · LAMP SHADE · MAGAZINES · EGG CARTONS · BANDAGES · PAPER MONEY

Hey Mom: Let's try this again

Graphic design makes unattractive copy **COME ALIVE.**

71 The number of million tons of paper and paperboard used each year. Some of those supplies are used to produce the 2 billion books, 350 million magazines, and 24 billion newspapers that are published annually.

6 UNIVERSAL COLOR HARMONIES

(clockwise, top) **COMPLEMENTARY**: colors are opposite from each other. **ANALOGOUS**: colors are right next to each other. **SPLIT-COMPLEMENTARY**: one base color plus two colors that on either side. **TRIADIC**: three colors evenly spaced around. **SQUARE**: four colors spaced evenly. (*finally*) **TETRADIC**: four colors in two complementary pairs.

12 KEYSTROKES FOR SPECIAL CHARACTERS

PUNCTUATION:
… ellipsis · option-;
' single open quote · option-]

6 VISUAL WAYS OF SHOWING INFORMATION

Right Page

THE GRAPHIC DESIGN EDITION
Featuring facts you ought to know, design sins, harmonious colors, who's who in type foundries, character gossip and books galore.
BY

Five **fab** typefaces

○ MRS. EAVES
Grumpy wizards make a toxic brew for the jovial queen.
Emigre/Zuzana Licko

○ AKZIDENZ GROTESK
Who on earth packed five dozen old quart jars in my box?
Berthold/Günter Gerhard Lange

○ CLARENDON
Few black taxis drive up major roads on quiet hazy nights.
Thorowgood/Robert Besley

○ TRADE GOTHIC
Back in June we delivered oxygen equipment of the same size.
Linotype/Jackson Burke

○ BODONI
My girl wove six dozen plaid jackets before she quit.
Berthold/Giambattista Bodoni

LEGEND
○ NAME · ○ IN A SENTENCE · ○ FOUNDRY AND DESIGNER

Products made from **recycled** materials

PAPER MONEY · GLOBES · NEWSPAPER · ENVELOPES · PENCILS · BANDAGES

Show and tell

PORTRAIT · TIMELINE · MAP · CHART · VARIABLE PLOT · FLOW CHART

Six laws of **visual** grouping

SIMILARITY · PROXIMITY · CONTINUITY · SYMMETRY · CLOSURE · SIMPLICITY

? DID YOU KNOW?
72 percent of newspaper and mechanical papers + 85 percent of corrugated cardboard were recovered in 2010.

Color harmony

 — COLOR WHEEL
 — COMPLEMENTARY
 — ANALOGOUS
 — SPLIT COMPLEMENTARY
 — TRIADIC

Five **valuable** books on design

KIMBERLY ELAM, *Typographic Systems of Design* (2007)
HELEN ARMSTRONG, *Graphic Design Theory* (2009)
ELLEN LUPTON, *Graphic Design Thinking: Beyond Brainstorming* (2011)
PHILLIP MEGGS, *The History of Graphic Design* (2011)
EMIL RUDER, *Typographie: A Manual of Design* (1967)

Unforgivable type crimes

But I must explain to you how all this mistaken idea of denouncing pleasure and praising pain was born and I will give you a complete account of the system and inadequacies and faults.

RIVERS

obtain it is pain.

DOUBLE SPACES

But I must explain to you mistaken idea of pleasure and pain and I will give you account of the

HIDEOUS RAGS

VILLAINS

Biodiagram In this project designers represent one facet of their lives according to a clear conceptual and visual framework. Form, color, and configuration must grow out of the hierarchy and nature of the content. Graduate Typography. Jennifer Cole Phillips, faculty.

Social Network This diagram details a complex array of Facebook activity for the month of August. In charting data such as likes, posts, and shares, the designer creates a snapshot of his social network and proclivities. Winner of a design excellence award from *Print Magazine*. Hieu Tran.

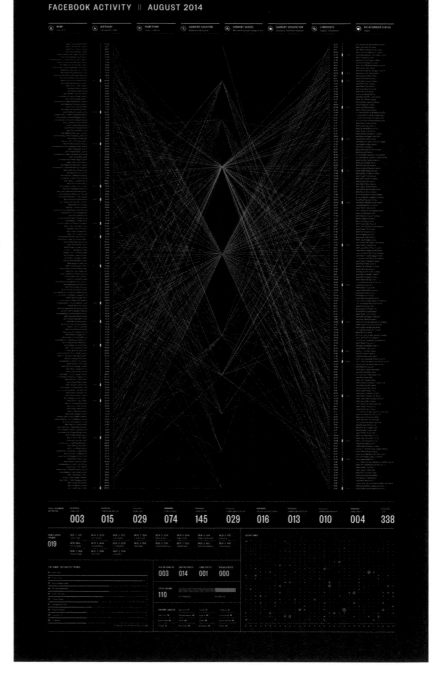

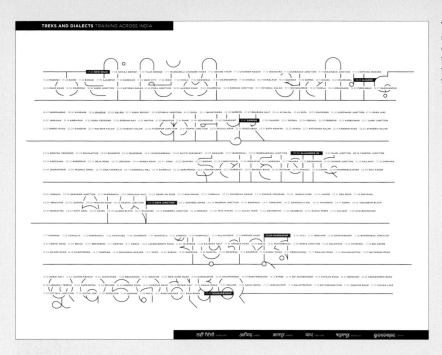

Train Tracking This diagram charts the seven shifting dialects encountered on a single train trip through India. The tiny type captures and records the towns traversed along the way, while the larger-level native changes by region. Hitesh Singhal.

Mercurial Moods This simple diagram charts the upward and downward trajectory of the designer's well-being based on specific forces that positively and negatively affect her world. Kajsa Nichols-Smith.

what affects my well-being

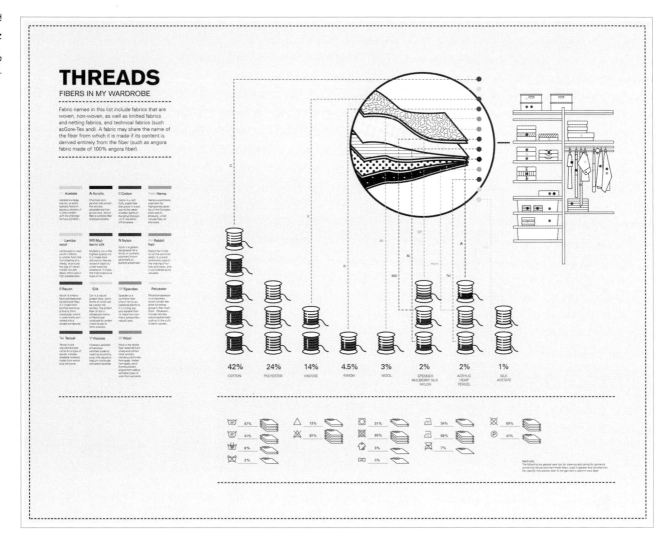

Fiber-enriched This intricate diagram dissects the fiber content of this designer's wardrobe and analyzes it according to a carefully articulated system of criteria. Wenji Lu.

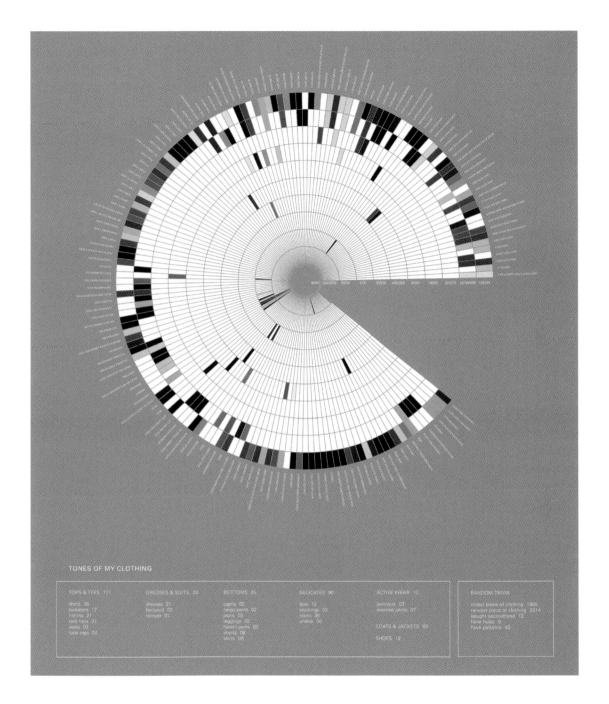

TONES OF MY CLOTHING

TOPS & TEES 111	DRESSES & SUITS 24	BOTTOMS 35	DELICATES 90	ACTIVE WEAR 10	RANDOM TRIVIA
shirts 38	dresses 21	capris 02	bras 12	swimsuit 03	oldest piece of clothing 1995
sweaters 17	bodysuit 02	cargo pants 02	stockings 03	exercise pants 07	newest piece of clothing 2014
t-shirts 21	romper 01	jeans 03	socks 36		bought secondhand 12
tank-tops 27		leggings 03	undies 39	COATS & JACKETS 03	have holes 9
vests 03		harem pants 02			have patterns 40
tube-tops 04		shorts 08		SHOES 12	
		skirts 09			

Color Snapshot A complex spectrum of color is mapped across every item in this designer's wardrobe. Clothing type is further broken down and classified by category and quantity. Tiffany Small.

Visualizing Marathon Launched in 2010 by visualizing.org, these annual marathons began in New York City as on-site twenty-four-hour student competitions, expanded to other on-site venues in major cities around the world, and finally invited global remote participation. Participants work in teams to visually illuminate given themes.

Cause + Effect Twenty teams from eight design schools were challenged to visualize the impact of humanity's footprint on Spaceship Earth at the inaugural Visualizing Marathon: a 24-hour student data visualization competition. MICA sent fourteen students to New York City to compete in the event and swept the competition, winning first place and honorable mention.

MICA's winning visualization, "One Day Cause + Effect," was lauded for its personal narrative and striking design and received the Jury's top score for "understanding"– the ability to help the reader better understand the impact of humanity's footprint on Earth. Chris Clark, Christina Beard, Supisa Wattanasanasanee, Chris McCampbell.

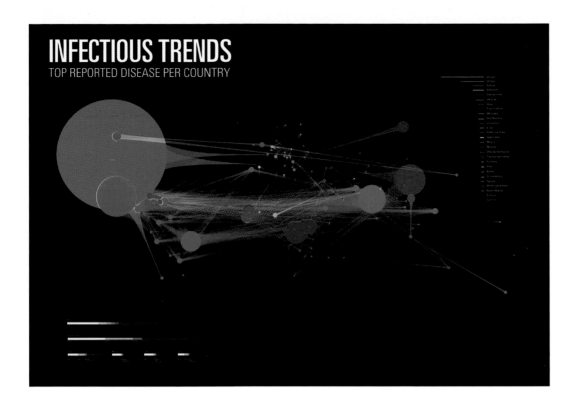

INFECTIOUS TRENDS
TOP REPORTED DISEASE PER COUNTRY

Infectious Trends This dynamic visualization charts the volume and network of global infectious diseases. Nicki Dlugash, Richard Blake, Qian Li.

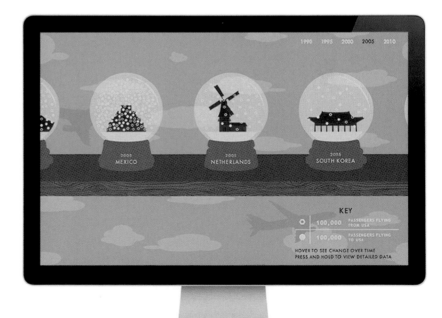

Around the Globe This interactive infographic uses snow globes to represent the amount of air traffic between the US and other countries over the past twenty years. Jackie Littman, Rob McConnell, Gabriela Hernandez, David Lam.

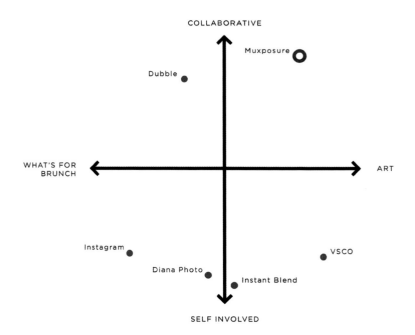

COLLABORATIVE

Muxposure

Dubble

WHAT'S FOR
BRUNCH

ART

Instagram

VSCO

Diana Photo

Instant Blend

SELF INVOLVED

Matrix Diagram Each axis in a matrix diagram represents a pair of opposing ideas. The diagram shown here explores the competitive landscape around a double-exposure photography app. The y axis contrasts collaborative with individual practice, while the x axis contrasts serious endeavors with casual "brunch" photos. The designer placed his product in the upper right: it is both collaborative and artistic. Alex Jacque.

Diagrams for Product Design

Creating digital products for people to use requires an understanding of structure, user flows, and relationships. Before visual design can begin, interaction designers have to look at the role of products within broader product ecosystems and consider the architecture of information and the narrative of use. Designers employ a variety of graphical tools to express these situations, from Venn diagrams and matrix charts to decision flows and wireframes. Product Design Workshop. Tim Hoover and Jessica Karle, faculty.

Game Play This diagram depicts the basic sequence of play in a game based on Dante's *Inferno*. The player strives to move up through the levels of Purgatory towards the ultimate goal of Paradise. This simple linear progression is disrupted when the player is sent to the bottom and forced to climb back out of Inferno. Nate Gulledge.

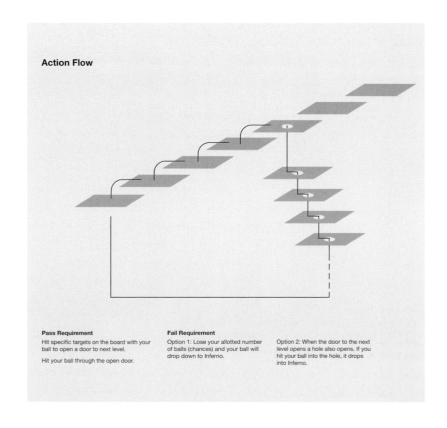

Action Flow

Pass Requirement
Hit specific targets on the board with your ball to open a door to next level.

Hit your ball through the open door.

Fail Requirement
Option 1: Lose your allotted number of balls (chances) and your ball will drop down to Inferno.

Option 2: When the door to the next level opens a hole also opens. If you hit your ball into the hole, it drops into Inferno.

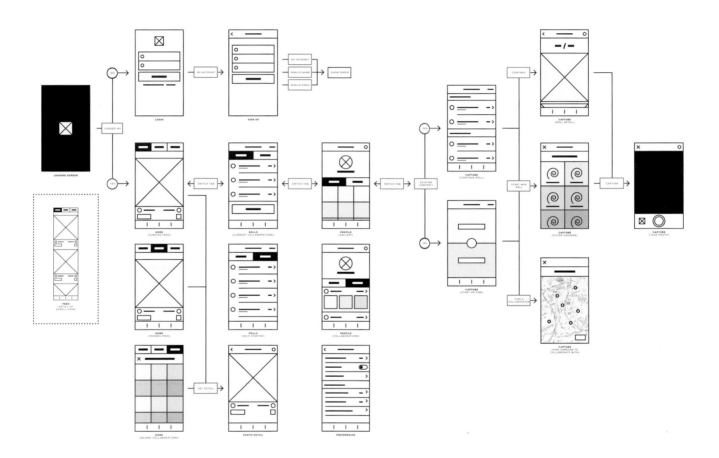

User Flow This sequence of wireframes for a photo app shows what happens when a user chooses different paths from the home screen. Many such paths are possible in a fully developed app. Alex Jacque.

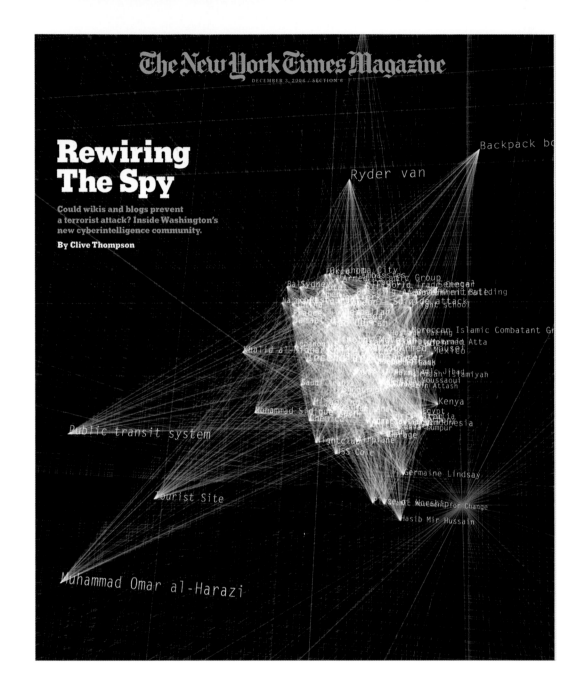

Underground Networks Created for the *New York Times Magazine* by media designer Lisa Strausfeld, this diagram visualizes complex relationships surrounding worldwide terrorist groups.

Produced using the computer language Processing, Strausfeld's diagram conveys the maddening difficulty involved in keeping track of countless potential links and dangers. Lisa Strausfeld, Pentagram.

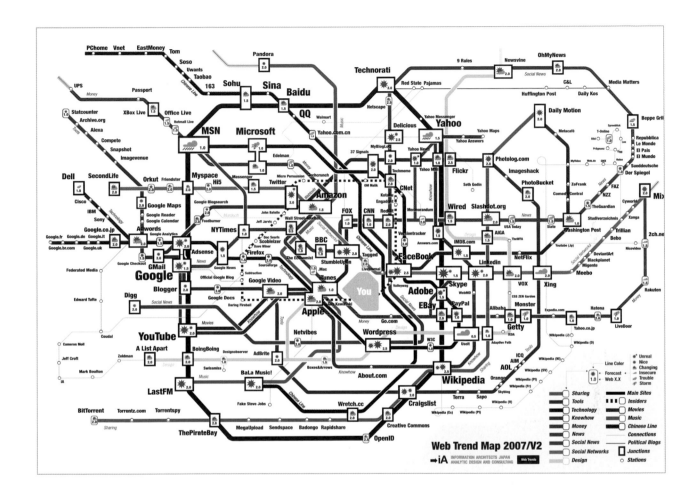

Charting Trends This seductive map selects and situates the world's two hundred most popular websites and classifies them according to categories such as design, music, moneymaking, and much more. The graphic is reminiscent of the subway map used in Tokyo, where this piece was designed. Information Architects.

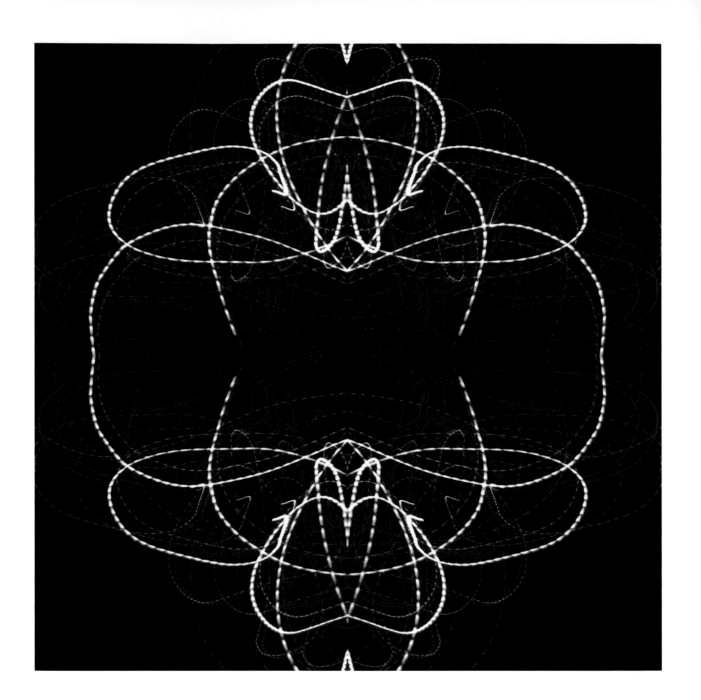

Time and Motion

Every drawing can be understood as a motion study
since it is **a path of motion** recorded by graphic means.

László Moholy-Nagy

Time and motion are closely related principles. Any word or image that moves functions both spatially and temporally. Motion is a kind of change, and change takes place in time. Motion can be implied as well as literal, however. Artists have long sought ways to represent the movement of bodies and the passage of time within the realm of static, two-dimensional space. Time and motion are considerations for all design work, from a multipage printed book, whose pages follow each other in time, to animations for film and television, which have literal duration.

Any still image has implied motion (or implied stasis), while motion graphics share compositional principles with print. Designers today routinely work in time-based media as well as print, and a design campaign often must function across multiple media simultaneously.

Animation encompasses diverse modes of visible change, including the literal movement of elements that fly on or off the screen as well as changes in scale, transparency, color, layer, and more. These alternative modes of change are especially useful for designing animated text on the web, where gratuitous movement can be more distracting than pleasing or informative.

It can be useful to think about the screen as an active, changing surface as well as a neutral stage or support onto which characters rush on and off. Thus a fixed field of dots, for example, can light up sequentially to spell out a message, or objects can become visible or invisible as the background behind them changes color or transparency. A word or design element can stay still while the environment around it changes.

Film is a visual art. Designers of motion graphics must think both like painters and typographers and like animators and filmmakers. A motion sequence is developed through a series of storyboards, which convey the main phases and movements of an animation. A style frame serves to establish the visual elements of a project, such as its colors, typefaces, illustrative components, and more. Such frames must be designed with the same attentiveness to composition, scale, color, and other principles as any work of design. In addition, the motion designer thinks about how all these components will change and interact with each other over time.

This chapter introduces some basic principles for conveying temporal change and motion, both in still and time-based media.

Long Exposure Photography A camera can capture a path of lights moving over time. The oscillations of AC currents are not visible to the eye, but, when recorded through a camera lens, the oscillations create a dashed line. DC currents generate smooth lines. Here, a single long-exposure photograph has been repeated and rotated to create a larger visual shape. Sarah Joy Jordahl Verville, MFA Studio.

Eruption of Form These shapes as well as their explosive arrangement suggest movement and change. Sasha Funk, Graphic Design I. Zvezdana Rogic, faculty.

Implied Motion

Graphic designers use numerous techniques to suggest change and movement on the printed page. Diagonal compositions evoke motion, while rectilinear arrangements appear static. Cropping a shape can suggest motion, as does a sinuous line or a pointed, triangular shape.

Static A centered object sitting parallel to the edges of the frame appears stable and unmoving.

Diagonal An object placed on a diagonal appears dynamic.

Cropped An object that is partly cut off appears to be moving into or out of the frame.

Point the Way The shape of an arrow indicates movement. Robert Ferrell and Geoff Hanssler, Digital Imaging. Nancy Froehlich, faculty.

Moment in Time A skilled photographer can capture a moving object at a dramatic instant. Steve Sheets, Digital Imaging. Nancy Froehlich, faculty.

Restless Line These scratchy, sketchy lines contrast with the static letterforms they describe. The letters were drawn with Processing code. Yeohyun Ahn, MFA Studio.

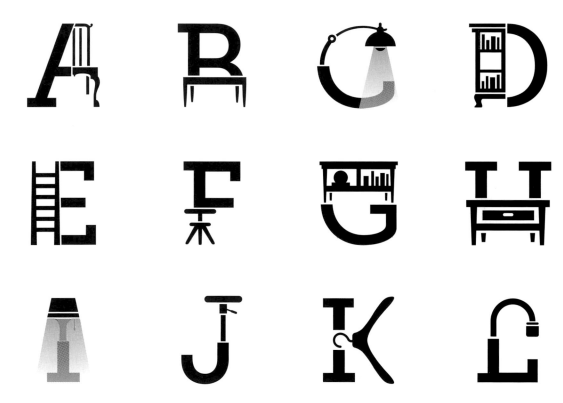

Animated Letters This alphabet is built from furniture parts. When set into motion as an animated GIF, the letters change. Legs break, drawers open, and lights turn on and off. Yushi Luo, Design Language Studio. Kiel Mutschelknaus, faculty.

A B C D

E F G H

I J K L

M N O P

Q R S T

Jiggle The sketches below for an animated typeface show how the designer planned the movement of these squishy letterforms. The final alphabet was produced as an animated GIF. Nate Gulledge, Design Language Studio. Kiel Mutschelknaus, faculty.

Type Worm The characters in this alarming
alphabet wiggle and jiggle like living things.
Light and shadow add to the unnerving
effect. Nick Emrich, Design Language Studio.
Kiel Mutschelknaus, faculty.

Implied Time and Motion An effective logotype can be applied to anything from a tiny business card to a large-scale architectural sign to a computer screen or digital projection. The logotypes shown here use a variety of graphic strategies to imply motion.

In this project, designers created a graphic identity for a conference about contemporary media art and theory called "Loop." Each solution explores the concept of the loop as a continuous, repeating sequence. The designers applied each logo to a banner in an architectural setting and to a screen-based looping animation. (Photoshop was used to simulate the installation of the banners in a real physical space.)

Jaime Bennati

Lindsay Orlowski

Loop Logo Numerous techniques are used in these studies of the word "loop" to imply movement and repetition. Some designs suggest the duration of the design process itself by exposing the interface or by drawing the logo with an endless, looping line. Above, transparency is used to create an onion-skin effect; cropping the logo on the banner further implies movement. Graphic Design II. Ellen Lupton, faculty.

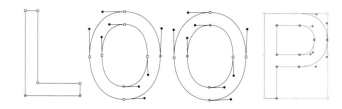

May Yang
Sueyun Choi
Lauretta Dolch

Alexandra Matzner
Lindsay Orlowski
Yuta Sakane

Change in Position Every object on a two-dimensional surface has a pair of x/y coordinates. Changing the coordinates moves the object. (3-D animation includes the z axis.) In this sequence, the object's x position is changing, while the y position is fixed, yielding a horizontal movement.

Change Over Time

All animation consists of change over time. The most obvious form of change consists of an element moving around on the screen—the Road Runner approach. The Road Runner can "walk" onto the screen like a character in a play, or it can appear there suddenly as in a cut in a film.

Changing the position of an object is just one way to make it change. Other modes of change include shifting its scale, color, shape, and transparency. By altering the degree of change and the speed with which the change takes place, the animator produces different qualities of movement. Complex and subtle behaviors are created by using different modes of change simultaneously. For example, an object can fade slowly onto the screen (changing transparency) while also getting bigger (changing in scale).

Change in Rotation Continuously altering the angle of an object creates the appearance of spinning, shaking, and other behaviors.

Change in Scale Making an object larger or smaller creates the impression of it moving backward or forward in space. Here, the object is not moving (changing its position); only its size is changing.

Change in Shape Letting a line wander can produce all types of shapes: abstract, amorphous, representational.

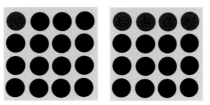
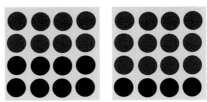
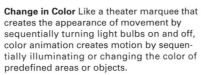

Change in Color Like a theater marquee that creates the appearance of movement by sequentially turning light bulbs on and off, color animation creates motion by sequentially illuminating or changing the color of predefined areas or objects.

Here, a wave of color appears to pass over a field of static objects. Countless variations are possible.

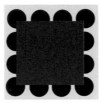

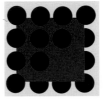
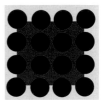

Change in Depth Many image-editing programs allow the designer to divide an image into layers, which are comparable to the sheets of transparent acetate used in traditional cell animation.

Layers can be duplicated, deleted, altered to support new image elements, merged into a single image, and hidden. Here, objects on back layers gradually move forward.

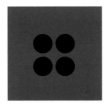
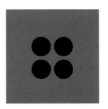
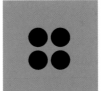

Change in Transparency Animators alter the transparency of an image to give it the appearance of fading in or out of view. Here, the top layer gradually becomes more transparent, revealing an image behind it.

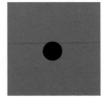
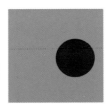

Multiple Modes of Change Most animations combine several modes of change at once.

This sequence incorporates changes in position, scale, color, and transparency.

Change in Position Moving text around the screen is the most basic means of animating type. Commonly, type enters from the right side of the screen and moves left to support the normal direction of reading. Ticker or leader text also tends to move in this direction.

Animating Type

In film and television and on the web, text is often in motion. Animating type is like animating other graphic elements, but the designer must pay special attention to legibility and reading order.

The most elementary technique is to shift the position of a word so that it appears to move around like a character or other object. Animated words do not have to literally move, however: they can fade in or fade out; they can flicker on or off the screen letter by letter; or they can change scale, color, layer, and so on.

When animating text, the designer adjusts the timing to make sure the words change slowly enough to be legible, but not so slowly that they become a drag to read. Context also is important. A constantly changing logo in a web banner, for example, will quickly become irritating, whereas sudden and constant motion in the title sequence of a film can help set the tone for the action to come.

Change in Color In the sequence shown here, the type itself is static, but a color change moves across the text letter by letter. Endless variations of this basic kind of change are possible.

Change in Transparency White type appears gradually on screen by gradually becoming opaque.

Multiple Modes of Change Many animations combine several techniques at once.

This sequence features change in position, scale, and transparency.

Time and Space Produced with Cinema 4D software, this animation was created by moving the virtual camera around 3D letterforms. Rendered in black and white, the animation is richly sculptural. Jamie Carusi, MFA Studio.

Storyboards

Since motion design can be labor-intensive, designers must plan carefully every aspect of a piece before production begins. Once a concept is developed, the script is fleshed out with storyboard sketches and a style frame. These visual tools are essential for designing commercials, online banners, television broadcast animations, and film title sequences.

Storyboards summarize the content or key moments of an animation's events. Storyboarding also determines the flow of the storyline and suggests the major changes of action. In addition to movements, the personality, emotions, and gestures of the characters and objects are also expressed. The layout of a storyboard, similar to that of a comic strip, consists of sketches or illustrations displayed sequentially to visualize an animated or live-action piece. Notes describing camera angles, soundtrack, movement, special effects, timing, and transitions between scenes are often included.

Style Frames

The ultimate look of an animation is expressed in one or more style frames, which set the aesthetic tone and formal elements. A style frame captures many of the graphic elements used throughout the piece. The typography, colors, patterns, illustrations, and photographs chosen for the project are often included.

Storyboarding and developing style frames are creative processes that allow the designer to plan and brainstorm before the animation is realized. These tools serve as guides to production and vehicles for presentation to clients. Successful style frames and storyboards are always clearly defined and easy to interpret.

Urban Life: Developing an Animation Late HIV diagnosis is common among immigrant Latino men despite the availability of free counseling and testing by bilingual health workers. The Baltimore City Health Department partnered with JHU Center for Clinical Global Health Education and the Center for Design Practice at MICA to produce a series of animated videos that address barriers such as inaccurate perception of risks, fear of testing, and lack of treatment knowledge. Designer Nate Gulledge used pencil sketches to develop a series of storyboards. After the narratives were approved, he built a cast of characters that employ basic shapes and a palette of rich, bright colors. Nate Gulledge, Center for Design Practice, MICA.

Urban Life: Animation Stills The designer used large type and changes in scale to create motion and drama with basic graphic elements. Nate Gulledge, Center for Design Practice, MICA.

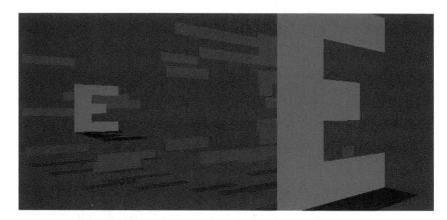

Beyond the Timeline

Interactive logos and graphics are another aspect of motion design. Rather than devising a narrative sequence with a fixed beginning and end, the interactive designer creates behaviors. These behaviors involve change over time, just like narrative animations, but they do not occur in a fixed sequence, and they are not designed using storyboards and timelines.

Interactive graphics are created with code, such as Flash ActionScript, Java, or Processing. Instead of working with the interface of a linear timeline, the designer writes functions, variables, if/then statements, and other instructions to define how the graphics will behave.

Interactive graphics need not be complex or hyperactive. Simple behaviors can delight users and enrich the experience of a digital interface. For example, an interactive logo on a webpage can wait quietly until it is touched with the user's mouse; instead of being an annoying distraction, the graphics come to life only when called upon to do so.

Letterscapes In these interactive graphics by Peter Cho, the letters dance, bounce, unravel, and otherwise transform themselves in response to mouse input. Peter Cho, 2002.

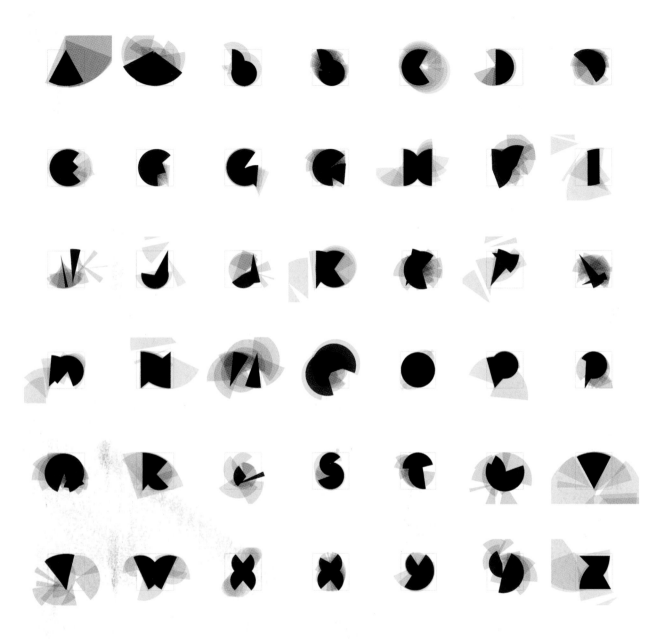

Type Me Again Simple pie shapes rotate
and repeat to create the letters of the
alphabet when users type in letters on their
keyboards. Peter Cho, 2000.

Rules and Randomness

The idea becomes a **machine** that makes the art. Sol LeWitt

Designers create rules as well as finished pieces. A magazine designer, for example, works with a grid and a typographic hierarchy that is interpreted in different ways, page after page, issue after issue. If the rules are well planned, other designers will be able to interpret them to produce their own unique and unexpected layouts. Rules create a framework for design without determining the end results.

Style sheets employed in print and web publishing (CSS) are rules for displaying the different parts of a document. By adjusting a style sheet, the designer can change the appearance of an entire book or website. Style sheets are used to reconfigure a single body of content for output in different media, from printed pages to the screen of a mobile phone.

Rules can be used to generate form as well as organize content. In the 1920s, the Bauhaus artist and designer László Moholy-Nagy created a painting by telephoning a set of instructions to a sign painter. In the 1960s, the minimalist artist Sol LeWitt created drawings based on simple instructions; the drawings could be executed on a wall or other surface anywhere in the world by following the directions. Complex webs of lines often resulted from seemingly simple verbal instructions.

Designers produce rules in computer code as well as natural language. C. E. B. Reas, who co-authored the software language Processing, creates rich digital drawings and interactive works that evolve from instructions and variables. Reas alters the outcome by changing the variables. He explains, "Sometimes I set strict rules, follow them, and then observe the results. More frequently, I begin with a core software behavior, implement it, and then observe the results. I then allow the piece to flow intuitively from there."[1] Reas and other contemporary artists are using software as a medium unto itself rather than as a tool supporting the design process.

Designing rules and instructions is an intrinsic part of the design process. Increasingly, designers are asked to create systems that other people will implement and that will change over time. This chapter looks at ways to use rule-based processes to generate unexpected visual results.

Unnatural Growth Created in Processing, this work by C. E. B. Reas resembles an organic process. The forms are created in response to rules governing the behavior of an initial set of points. The work builds over time as the program runs through its iterations. C. E. B. Reas. *Process 6 (Image 3)*, 2005 (detail).

1. C. E. B. Reas, "Process/Drawing," (Statement for the exhibition at the bitforms gallery, New York, March 4–April 2, 2005).

Numbers are replaced with icons from different symbol fonts. Marleen Kuijf.

Strange hieroglyphs are created by doubling and flipping each numeral. Katie Evans.

Cell Phone Symphony In the project shown here, students were given a list of phone numbers from which to generate visual imagery for a poster. The posters promote a "cell phone symphony," featuring music composed via interaction among the audience's cell phones.

Each poster suggests auditory experience as well as ideas of social and technological interaction. The students took numerous different approaches, from turning each phone number into a linear graph to using the digits to set the size and color of objects in a grid.

Designing the system is part of the creative process. The visual results have an organic quality that comes from random input to the system. The designer controls and manipulates the system itself rather than the final outcome. Graphic Design II. Ellen Lupton, faculty.

Numbers are used to set the color and size of dots on a grid. Hayley Griffin.

Each ten-digit number is a linear graph.
Martina Novakova.

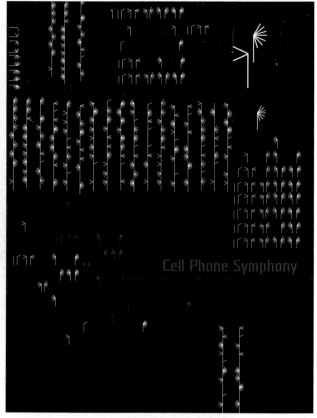

Each phone number is a twig that sprouts
marks for its digits. Martina Novakova.

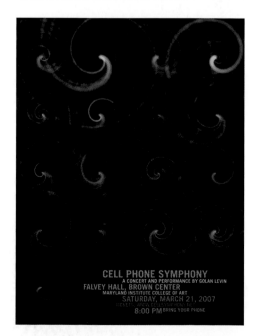

Computer code is used to create a spiraling
path for each number. Jonnie Hallman.

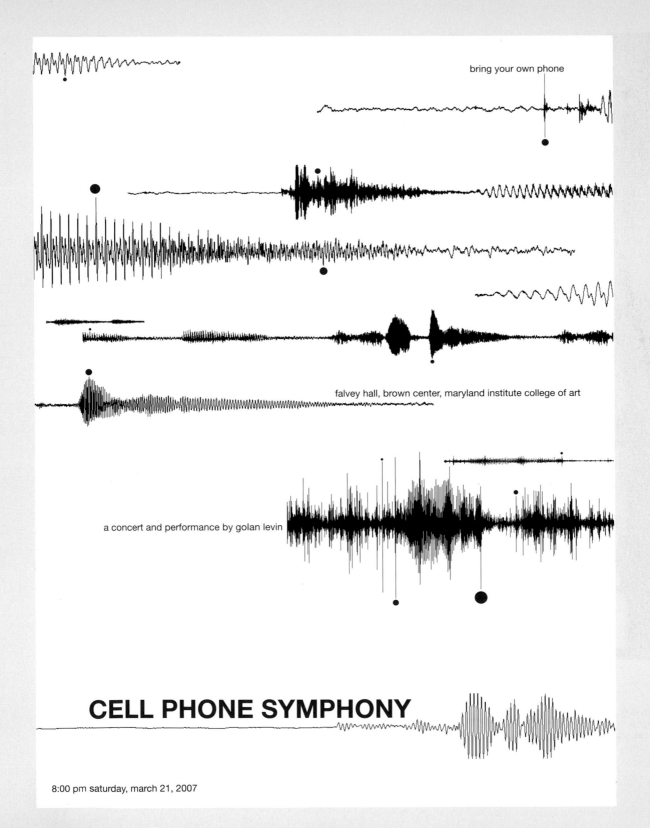

bring your own phone

falvey hall, brown center, maryland institute college of art

a concert and performance by golan levin

CELL PHONE SYMPHONY

8:00 pm saturday, march 21, 2007

Audio Waves Captured from an audio editing program, the lines represent different voices speaking a list of phone numbers. Sisi Recht.

Photoshop Actions To create this series of posters, the designer recorded actions in Photoshop. Each time the action runs using different parameters, the system generates different results. Lolo Zhang, DesignLanguage Studio. Kiel Mutschelknaus, faculty.

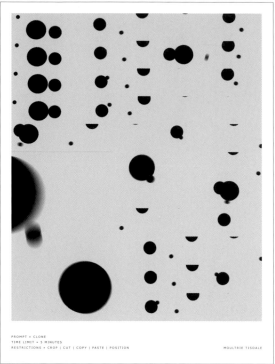

PROMPT • CLONE
TIME LIMIT • 5 MINUTES
RESTRICTIONS • CROP | CUT | COPY | PASTE | POSITION   MOULTRIE TISDALE

Moultrie Tisdale

Motion Prompt How can time and motion be represented on a flat surface? Designers created a series of "gesture studies" in InDesign based on provided templates and using fifty-five frames from an animated shapes project they were already working on. Each template contained a prompt (such as morph, deface, contain, clone, pulverize), a series of constraints (such as copy, paste, cut, and position), and a time limit (one minute to several minutes). Each designer sought to capture the spirit of the prompt within the set constraints. They were asked to embrace motion graphics software not just as a way to generate animations, but as a way to generate material for developing two-dimensional imagery. Graphic Design III. Jason Gottleib and Kristian Bjørnard, faculty.

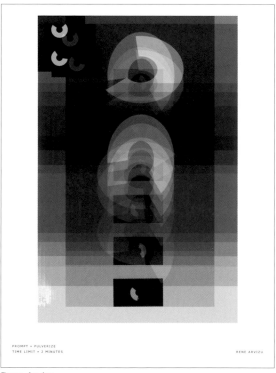

PROMPT • PULVERIZE
TIME LIMIT • 2 MINUTES   RENE ARVIZU

Rene Arvizu

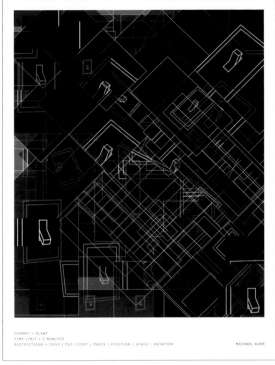

PROMPT + SLANT
TIME LIMIT + 3 MINUTES
RESTRICTIONS + CROP | CUT | COPY | PASTE | POSITION | SCALE | ROTATION   MICHAEL AUER

Michael Auer

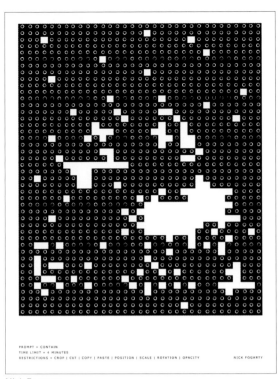

PROMPT + CONTAIN
TIME LIMIT + 4 MINUTES
RESTRICTIONS + CROP | CUT | COPY | PASTE | POSITION | SCALE | ROTATION | OPACITY   NICK FOGARTY

Nick Fogarty

PROMPT + DEFACE
TIME LIMIT + 3 MINUTES   JEFF MILLS

Jeff Mills

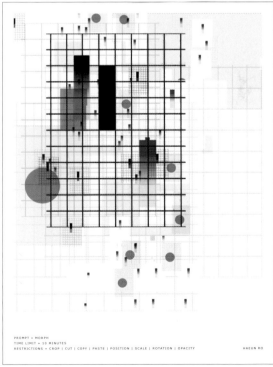

PROMPT + MORPH
TIME LIMIT + 10 MINUTES
RESTRICTIONS + CROP | CUT | COPY | PASTE | POSITION | SCALE | ROTATION | OPACITY   HAEUN RO

Haeun Ro

Yeohyun Ahn

Repeat and Rotate

Repeating and rotating forms are universal principles of pattern design. The designs shown here were created in the Processing software language. By altering the input to a set of digital instructions, the designer can quickly see numerous variations of a single design. Changing the typeface, type size, type alignment, color, transparency, and the number and degree of rotations yields different results.

```
for(int i=0;i<12;i++){
fill(0,0,0);
textAlign(CENTER);
pushMatrix();

rotate(PI*i/6);

text("F",0,0);
popMatrix();
}
}
```

Similar effects can be achieved by rotating and repeating characters in standard graphics programs such as Illustrator. Working in Processing or other code languages allows the designer to test and manipulate different variables while grasping the logic and mathematics behind pattern design.

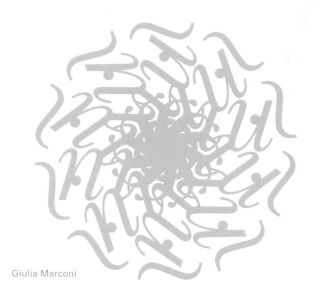

Giulia Marconi

Giulia Marconi

Rotated Letterforms A simple code structure is used to generate designs with surprising intricacy. New designs can be quickly tested by changing the variables. Graphic Design II. Ellen Lupton and Yeohyun Ahn, faculty.

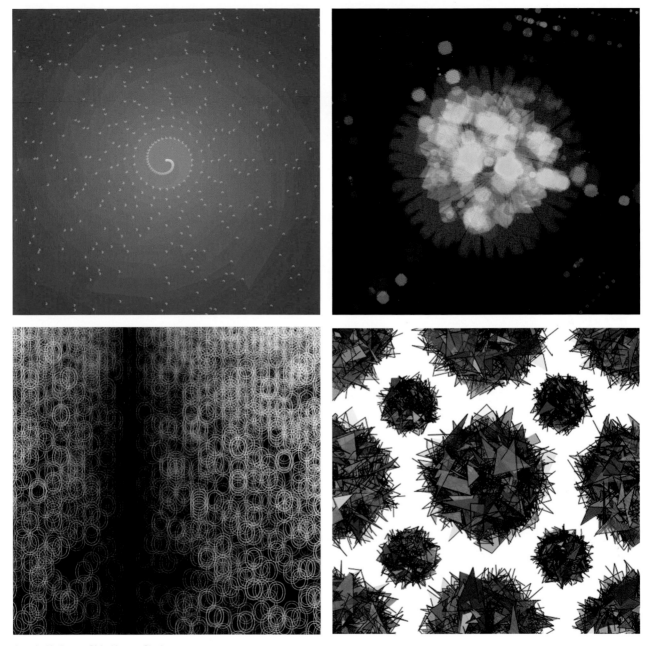

Jonnie Hallman, Shin Hyung Choi

Jessica Till, Adam Okrasinski

Repeat and Random One or two simple
elements are repeated using a "for" statement.
The transparency, size, or x and y coordinates
are randomized to create a sense of natural
motion. Graphic Design II. Ellen Lupton and
Yeohyun Ahn, faculty.

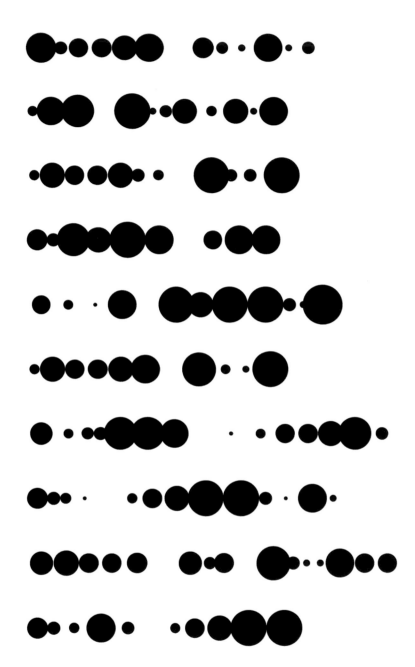

Abstract Alphabet The Latin alphabet is an inherently abstract code. To create this minimal typeface, the designer replaced letterforms with dots of varying size. Although rendered illegible, the resulting texts maintain a familiar sense of rhythm. Kirby Matherne, Design Language Studio. Kiel Mutschelknaus, faculty.

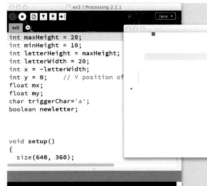

```
int maxHeight = 20;
int minHeight = 10;
int letterHeight = maxHeight;
int letterWidth = 20;
int x = -letterWidth;
int y = 0;      // Y position of
float mx;
float my;
char triggerChar='a';
boolean newletter;


void setup()
{
  size(640, 360);
```

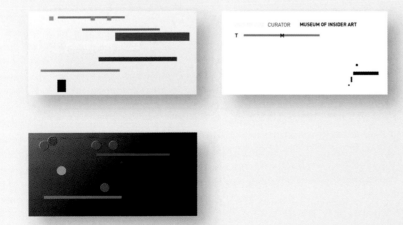

Museum of Insider Art To create a visual brand for an imaginary museum, the designer created a code in Processing that converts alphabetic characters into abstract shapes. The shapes become a private code. Wenjie Lu, MFA Studio.

Bibliography

Basics

Arnheim, Rudolf. *Visual Thinking*. Berkeley: University of California Press, 1969.

Arnston, Amy. *Graphic Design Basics*. New York: Holt Rinehart and Winston, 1988.

Blauvelt, Andrew and Ellen Lupton, eds. *Graphic Design: Now In Production*. Minneapolis: Walker Art Center, 2011.

Booth-Clibborn, Edward, and Daniele Baroni. *The Language of Graphics*. New York: Harry N. Abrams, 1979.

Carter, Rob, Ben Day, and Phillip Meggs. *Typographic Design: Form and Communication*. New York: Wiley, 2002. First published 1985.

Dondis, Donis. *A Primer of Visual Literacy*. Cambridge, MA: MIT Press, 1973.

Garland, Ken. *Graphics Handbook*. New York: Reinhold, 1966.

Graham, Lisa. *Basics of Design: Layout and Typography for Beginners*. Florence, KY: Thomson Delmar Learning, 2001.

Grear, Malcolm. *Inside/Outside: From the Basics to the Practice of Design*. New York: AIGA and New Riders, 2006.

Hofmann, Armin. *Graphic Design Manual: Principles and Practice*. New York: Reinhold, 1966.

Kandinsky, Wassily. *Point and Line to Plane*. New York: Dover, 1979.

Klee, Paul. *Pedagogical Sketchbook*. London: Faber and Faber, 1953.

Koren, Leonard, and R. Wippo Meckler. *The Graphic Design Cookbook: Mix and Match Recipes for Faster, Better Layouts*. San Francisco: Chronicle Books, 2001.

Krause, Jim. *Layout Index*. Cincinnati, OH: North Light Books, 2001.

Landa, Robin. *Graphic Design Solutions*. Florence, KY: OnWord Press, 2000.

Leborg, Christian. *Visual Grammar*. New York: Princeton Architectural Press, 2006.

Newark, Quentin. *What is Graphic Design?* East Sussex, UK: RotoVision, 2002.

Rand, Paul. *Paul Rand: A Designer's Art*. New Haven: Yale University Press, 1985.

Resnick, Elizabeth. *Design for Communication: Conceptual Graphic Design Basics*. New York: Wiley, 2003.

Rüegg, Ruedi. *Basic Typography: Design with Letters*. New York: Van Nostrand Reinhold, 1989.

Skolos, Nancy, and Thomas Wedell. *Type, Image, Message: A Graphic Design Layout Workshop*. Gloucester, MA: Rockport Publishers, 2006.

White, Alex. *The Elements of Graphic Design: Space, Unity, Page Architecture, and Type*. New York: Allworth Press, 2002.

Wilde, Richard, and Judith Wilde. *Visual Literacy: A Conceptual Approach to Graphic Problem-Solving*. New York: Watson-Guptill, 2005.

Williams, Robin. *The Non-Designer's Design Book*. Berkeley, CA: Peachpit Press, 2003.

Code

Dawes, Brendan. *Analog In, Digital Out: Brendan Dawes on Interaction Design*. Berkeley, CA: New Riders Press, 2006.

Gerstner, Karl. *Designing Programmes*. Zurich: ABC Verlag, 1963.

Maeda, John. *Creative Code*. London: Thames and Hudson, 2004.

Reas, Casey, Ben Fry, and John Maeda. *Processing: A Programming Handbook for Visual Designers and Artist*. Cambridge, MA: MIT Press, 2007.

Reas, C. E. B. *Process/Drawing*. Berlin: DAM, 2005.

Color

AdamsMorioka and Terry Stone. *Color Design Workbook: A Real-World Guide to Using Color in Graphic Design*. Gloucester, MA: Rockport Press, 2006.

Albers, Josef. *Interaction of Color*. New Haven: Yale University Press, 2006. First published 1963.

Krause, Jim. *Color Index*. Cincinnati: How Design Books, 2002.

Kuehni, Rolf G., and Andreas Schwarz. *Color Ordered: A Survey of Color Order Systems from Antiquity to the Present*. Oxford; New York: Oxford University Press, 2008.

Diagram

Bertin, Jacques. *Semiology of Graphics*. Madison, Wis.: University of Wisconsin Press, 1983.

Bhaskaran, Lakshmi. *Size Matters: Effective Graphic Design for Large Amounts of Information*. Mies, Switzerland: RotoVision, 2004.

Eisner, Will. *Graphic Storytelling and Visual Narrative*. New York: W. W. Norton & Company, 2008.

Tufte, Edward R. *Beautiful Evidence*. Cheshire, CT: Graphics Press, 2006.

———. *Envisioning Information*. Cheshire, CT: Graphics Press, 1990.

Grid

Bosshard, Hans Rudolf. *Der Typografische Raster/The Typographic Grid*. Sulgen, Switzerland: Verlag Niggli, 2000.

Elam, Kimberly. *Geometry of Design*. New York: Princeton Architectural Press, 2001.

———. *Grid Systems: Principles of Organizing Type*. New York: Princeton Architectural Press, 2005.

Jute, André. *Grids: The Structure of Graphic Design*. Mies, Switzerland: RotoVision, 1996.

Müller-Brockmann, Josef. *Grid Systems in Graphic Design*. Santa Monica, CA: RAM Publications, 1996. First published 1961.

Samara, Timothy. *Making and Breaking the Grid: A Graphic Design Layout Workshop*. Gloucester, MA: Rockport Publishers, 2002.

History and Theory

Alexander, Christopher. "The City is Not a Tree." In *Architecture Culture, 1943–1968: A Documentary Anthology*, edited by Joan Ockman. New York: Rizzoli, 1993, 379–88.

Arnheim, Rudolf. *Art and Visual Perception*. Berkeley: University of California Press, 1974.

Armstrong, Helen. *Graphic Design Theory: Readings from the Field*. New York: Princeton Architectural Press, 2009.

Crow, David. *Visible Signs. An Introduction to Semiotics in the Visual Arts*. Lausanne: AVA Academia, 2010.

Davis, Meredith. *Graphic Design Theory*. London: Thames & Hudson, 2012.

Derrida, Jacques. *The Truth in Painting*. Translated by Geoff Bennington and Ian McCleod. Chicago: University of Chicago Press, 1987.

Fish, Stanley. "Devoid of Content." *New York Times*. May 31, 2005, Op-Ed page.

Franciscono, Marcel. *Walter Gropius and the Creation of the Bauhaus*. Urbana: University of Illinois Press, 1971.

Galloway, Alexander, and Eugene Thacker. "Protocol, Control and Networks." *Grey Room* 12 (2004): 6–29.

Haverkamp, Michael. *Synesthetic Design: Handbook for a Multi-Sensory Approach*. Basel: Birkhäuser, 2011.

Heller, Steven, and Véronique Vienne. *100 Ideas That Changed Graphic Design*. London: Laurence King Publishing Ltd., 2012.

Itten, Johannes. *Design and Form: The Basic Course at the Bauhaus and Later*. New York: Van Nostrand Reinhold, 1975.

Johnson, Steven. *Everything Bad Is Good for You: How Today's Popular Culture is Actually Making Us Smarter*. New York: Penguin, 2005.

Kepes, Gyorgy. *Language of Vision*. Chicago: Paul Theobold, 1947.

Lupton, Ellen and J. Abbott Miller. *Design Writing Research: Writing on Graphic Design*. London: Phaidon, 1999.

Manovich, Lev. "Generation Flash." http://www.manovich.net (accessed May 10, 2006).

———. *The Language of New Media*. Cambridge, MA: MIT Press, 2001.

Margolin, Victor. *The Struggle for Utopia: Rodchenko, Lissitzky, Moholy-Nagy, 1917–1946*. Chicago: University of Chicago Press, 1998.

McCoy, Katherine. "Hybridity Happens." *Emigre* 67 (2004): 38–47.

———. "The New Discourse." In *Cranbrook: The New Design Discourse*, by Katherine McCoy and Michael McCoy. New York: Rizzoli, 1990.

———. "When Designers Create Culture." *Print* LVI: III (2002): 26, 181–3.

Moholy-Nagy, László. *Vision in Motion*. Chicago: Paul Theobold, 1969. First published 1947.

Moholy-Nagy, Sibyl. *Moholy-Nagy: Experiment in Totality*. Cambridge, MA: MIT Press, 1950.

Naylor, Gillian. *The Bauhaus Reassessed*. New York: E. P. Dutton, 1985.

Rowe, Colin, and Robert Slutzky. "Transparency: Literal and Phenomenal (Part 2)." In *Architecture Culture, 1943–1968: A Documentary Anthology*, edited by Joan Ockman. New York: Rizzoli, 1993, 205–225.

Weber, Nicholas Fox. *Josef + Anni Albers: Designs for Living*. London: Merrell Publishers, 2004.

Weingart, Wolfgang. *My Way to Typography*. Baden, Switzerland: Lars Müller Publishers, 2000.

Wick, Rainer K., and Gabriele D. Grawe. *Teaching at the Bauhaus*. Ostfildern-Ruit, Germany: Hatje Cantz Publishers, 2000.

Wingler, Hans M. *The Bauhaus*. Cambridge, MA: MIT Press, 1986.

Pattern

Archibald Christie. *Traditional Methods of Pattern Designing; An Introduction to the Study of the Decorative Art*. Oxford: Clarendon Press, 1910.

Hagan, Keith. *The Complete Pattern Library*. New York: Harry N. Abrams, 2005.

Jones, Owen. *The Grammar of Ornament*. Edited by Maxine Lewis. London: DK Adult, 2001. First published 1856.

Time and Motion

Furniss, Maureen. *Art in Motion: Animation Aesthetics*. London: John Libbey, 1998.

Moggridge, Bill. *Designing Interactions*. Cambridge, MA: The MIT Press, 2007.

Williams, Richard. *The Animator's Survival Kit: A Manual of Methods, Principles, and Formulas for Classical, Computer, Games, Stop Motion and Internet Animators*. London: Faber and Faber, 2001.

Woolman, Matt, and Jeff Bellantoni. *Moving Type: Designing for Time and Space*. Mies, Switzerland: RotoVision, 2000.

Typography

Baines, Phil, and Andrew Haslam. *Type and Typography*. New York: Watson-Guptill Publications, 2002.

Bringhurst, Robert. *The Elements of Typographic Style*. Vancouver: Hartley and Marks, 1997.

Carter, Rob, Ben Day, and Philip Meggs. *Typographic Design: Form and Communication*. New York: Van Nostrand Reinhold, 1993.

Elam, Kimberly. *Typographic Systems*. New York: Princeton Architectural Press, 2007.

Kane, John. *A Type Primer*. London: Laurence King, 2002.

Kunz, Willi. *Typography: Formation and Transformation*. Sulgen, Switzerland: Verlag Niggli, 2003.

———. *Typography: Macro- and Microaesthetics*. Sulgen, Switzerland: Verlag Niggli, 2004.

Lupton, Ellen. *Thinking with Type, Second Edition: A Critical Guide for Designers, Writers, Editors, and Students*. New York: Princeton Architectural Press, 2010.

Lupton, Ellen, ed. *Type on Screen: A Critical Guide for Designers, Writers, Developers, and Students*. New York: Princeton Architectural Press, 2014.

Ruder, Emil. *Typography*. New York: Hastings House, 1971.

Spiekermann, Erik, and E. M. Ginger. *Stop Stealing Sheep and Find Out How Type Works*. Mountain View, CA: Adobe Press, 1993.

Index

Student Contributors

Colophon

Book Typography
Univers family, designed by Adrian Frutiger, 1957

Cover Typography
Knockout, designed by Jonathan Hoefler, 1993–1997